"I thoroughly enjoyed reading your book. Your knowledge and insights are very clear, as is your passion for this market and issue. I think your comments about regulation are appropriate. First, a financially sound clearinghouse is necessary to provide the confidence for any firms, traders and farmers to participate. Secondly, a government authority is necessary to oversee and prevent abuse by any trader or group of traders. I realize you are advocating a step-by-step approach. The Chinese government must move to a farm system that allows farmers to plant based on what the market needs. Price should guide the allocation of resources, namely, land and water. This is the first step and the priority."

RALPH DER ASADOURIAN
Former Regulator at the CFTC in Chicago.

"Your book is very good, Milo, extremely well written and interesting to anyone in the rice trade for sure. It is educational and a good recap of history coupled to present day happenings in this ever-narrowing world. Things are moving quickly and I won't be surprised to see quite a few changes in global rice paradigms. Perhaps your book will help open the door and ease people's minds about what is to come. All this is going to happen one way or the other."

RANDY OUZTS
General Manager
Horizon Ag LLC
Memphis, TN

"I just finished your book, a great job. It was very insightful, especially the potentially disruptive impacts of a lost rice industry in China. Your years of study and practice shine. I will recommend the book to others and we must keep you in mind for one of our upcoming conferences as a speaker."

BRUCE SCHERR
Chairman of the Board • Chief Executive Officer
Informa Economics, Inc.
Memphis, Tennessee

"Thank you for your book, When Rice Shakes the World. *I have read it and enjoyed it and appreciate your thoughts."*

MR. GROVER CONNELL
The Connell Company
Berkeley Heights, New Jersey

"I just finished reading your book, and I have to congratulate you, it is a fantastic read!! You write so well, it was effortless for me to read. I started reading it on Sunday and couldn't put it down. There are so many thought provoking and insightful comments throughout. I've got to say I learned a lot—your book educates and entertains. You really paint an interesting picture of what is likely to happen in rice markets, China, and other Asian economies in the future. You tie in the water issues very well and offer well thought out solutions of how to mend Asia's broken rice markets. Bottom line, I agree the Asian rice markets need a futures contract and that it will happen. When I wrote my ADB report I was in no doubt as to the need for and the benefits of a contract, but I was pessimistic as to its likely success in the immediate term, given the heavy government price intervention in the region. However, having read your book I feel optimistic that a contract must develop sometime in the future. I hadn't thought about starting with a buffer stock in Singapore that would trade a milled contract. Also, I think I underestimated the power of the Internet to open up trading and price transparency—you make this point very well. I honestly don't think anyone else could have written this story any better. You are somewhat unique as you are able to bridge the gap between industry, academia and politics. I believe this book should have a very wide audience—it's a good read, not just for people already interested in rice."

PROFESSOR ANDREW MCKENZIE

Agricultural Economics and Agribusiness
Dale Bumpers College of Agricultural, Food, and Life Science
University of Arkansas
Fayetteville, Arkansas

"As one of the world's leading experts on rice and a former colleague early in our careers, Milo Hamilton makes a stirring case in this book that the greatest advancements in human history have not so much been advances in knowledge and technology, but recognition of where that comes from—the power of the human spirit and intellect when properly motivated, incentivized and unleashed."

DAN MANTERNACH

Director of Operations
Doane Advisory Services
St. Louis, Missouri

"*Milo Hamilton is well versed in the business of rice globally and we read his weekly rice newsletter for the prices and insight contained in it. When Rice Shakes the World is worth reading for all those who want a better understanding of trends in the world rice industry. It also presents some of the problems that China must face in dealing with all the change that lies ahead. It is well written and it is written from the heart, which is important. He has done a great job. Congratulations and cheers.*"

MS. HU WENZHONG
Agricultural Economist and Rice Specialist
Beijing, China

"*I learned a lot from Milo Hamilton's book and it also left me with a lot of questions. He is a great story teller with a passion for rice and the Asian rice farmer. I did not know about the emergence of agricultural futures in the USA. He makes a convincing argument for the farmer, not governments, managing food security in Asia and that this is a road to prosperity for the farmer as well. I plan to register for the merchandising course he mentioned. I feel I have much to learn. The Pakistani farmer has much more business savvy than many in Asia. His book was a pleasure to read.*"

SHAHID TARER
Galaxy Rice Mill
Gujranwala, Pakistan

"*Milo Hamilton is in a unique position to speak about this subject. This book is a culmination of his experience in almost every facet of the rice industry and it gives the reader an understanding of the culture, political and socioeconomic challenges that exist in the industry. Not only does he frame the issue, but he also offers his solution that is truly a win-win for everyone. As someone who teaches merchandising, farm marketing and hedging as a profession, I can unequivocally say that Milo is spot-on in his assertions of how to improve and fortify the global rice industry for generations to come. To top it off, the book is written masterfully. It is easy to read, understand and leaves you wanting to go and tell people all about it.*"

JASON WHEELER
Grain Merchandising Specialist
White Commercial Corporation
Stuart, Florida

"I found Milo Hamilton's book a very interesting read and it reflects the direction in which I think the world rice industry should move. Everything is currently very finely balanced and the warning signs that something might tip that balance significantly are there for all to see. I hope this book is well received as it is the kind of educational literature necessary to accurately commoditise rice. I enjoyed how you illustrated the inextricable link between rice and water. I am so much more aware now that when China or Nigeria import rice they are actually importing water as well. We at the Live Rice Index believe that price discovery is positive for market participants and that 'transparency' does not mean 'reduced income'. Yes, margins may be squeezed somewhat but worldwide traded volumes could explode if paper contracts are developed for rice, thereby improving risk management options and increasing opportunities to secure margins. If there is any way that we can collaborate in this educational endeavour then we are all ears. We wish this book all the best in its efforts to find a better way to trade rice."

STEPHEN JONES
Managing Director
Live Rice Index
United Kingdom

"Milo Hamilton's new book, When Rice Shakes the World, *has a wealth of insight on trends in the rice market and how rice and water are tied together. I read his newsletter with great interest and it is helpful to have a book to further understand his view of the future of the world rice market. No one else I know of has as much trading and commercial experience and is talking about the shape of the rice world to come. If you are concerned about rice, read his book!"*

PHAM QUANG DIEU
Founder and President
Agrimonitor,
Hanoi, Vietnam

"I appreciate the drive behind this book. Perhaps Milo Hamilton does not know it but this helps me prepare the next generation that will run my farms. It gives them a bigger perspective for their efforts. The book is good and hopefully will be read by many. I now realize the potential influence of it when I was fielding questions from my son, Caleb, and Josh, my son-in-law who is working with us now on the farm. These were questions raised after they came into contact with his ideas."

DEAN WALL
Rice Farmer,
Walnut Ridge, AR

WHEN RICE SHAKES THE WORLD

Tim

Enjoy my rice story.

Regards

[signature]

June 2014

WHEN RICE SHAKES THE WORLD

THE IMPORTANCE OF THE FIRST GRAIN
TO WORLD ECONOMIC & POLITICAL STABILITY

MILO HAMILTON

Former Rice Procurement Manager, Uncle Ben's, Inc.
and
Co-founder, Firstgrain.com©

Published by Advantage, Charleston, South Carolina.
Member of Advantage Media Group.

ADVANTAGE is a registered trademark and the Advantage colophon is a trademark of Advantage Media Group, Inc.

Printed in the United States of America.

ISBN: 978-159932-398-5
LCCN: 2001012345

This publication is designed to provide accurate and authoritative information in regard to the subject matter covered. It is sold with the understanding that the publisher is not engaged in rendering legal, accounting, or other professional services. If legal advice or other expert assistance is required, the services of a competent professional person should be sought.

 Advantage Media Group is proud to be a part of the Tree Neutral® program. Tree Neutral offsets the number of trees consumed in the production and printing of this book by taking proactive steps such as planting trees in direct proportion to the number of trees used to print books. To learn more about Tree Neutral, please visit www.treeneutral.com. To learn more about Advantage's commitment to being a responsible steward of the environment, please visit www.advantagefamily.com/green

Advantage Media Group is a publisher of business, self-improvement, and professional development books and online learning. We help entrepreneurs, business leaders, and professionals share their Stories, Passion, and Knowledge to help others Learn & Grow. Do you have a manuscript or book idea that you would like us to consider for publishing? Please visit advantagefamily.com or call 1.866.775.1696.

This book is dedicated to my wife, Jan, and my business partner, Kevin, and our two families.

With gratitude, we share the privilege of working with our rice customers. You are an awesome bunch and you inspire me greatly.

"The obstacle is the way."
—ZEN PROVERB

•

"Allowing farmers to sell their residential land rights to urban buyers is a small but important step towards unifying the rural and urban land markets. And enabling farmers to mortgage their land by providing land-use rights as collateral will help farmers unlock some of the dormant value in their land. Yet individual farmers still cannot sell the land they till, because it is not theirs to sell. It is indefensible that urban citizens should enjoy full individual property rights while farmers remain chained to the village collective. Collective ownership has patently failed to protect farmers from scheming local officials and village cadres. Any discussion of private ownership remains political dynamite, but the only logical trajectory of reform is to give individual farmers more rights over their land."
—TOM MILLER, CHINA'S URBAN BILLION: THE STORY BEHIND THE BIGGEST MIGRATION IN HUMAN HISTORY

•

"If you farm as a way of life, it will become expensive; but if you farm as a business, it can be a very rewarding way of life."
—MERRILL OSTER, FOUNDER OF PROFESSIONAL FARMERS OF AMERICA

TABLE OF CONTENTS

THE PURPOSE OF THIS BOOK

*R*ice farming in Asia must move from the eighteenth century into the twenty-first century in the next two decades, or the world as we know it could come unhinged. Grain prices could skyrocket, interest rates rise, and the Western economy brought to its knees by this simple white grain that feeds so many.

If you live in the West, what does your life have to do with the price of rice in China? A generation ago, not much, but today the fate of rice farms in China could improve or threaten the world economy. Here is why.

Rice is just not another pretty grain commodity tracked in the *Wall Street Journal.* Rice and the water in which it is grown are on the move — and hopefully so is the mindset of many in Asia who will control the outcome of this fascinating story. Being aware of what we cannot control can be just as important as knowing what we can control. You cannot control or predict earthquakes, but you need to know if you live over a deadly fault line.

Rice is a side dish and a commodity grown for cash in the West. In China and much of Asia, it is a way of life, farmed by peasants making less than $2 per day. China is the largest buyer and seller of rice in the world. Due to its vast ownership of assets and debt in the West, China's stability is essential to world economic stability. Many worry about the social unrest in urban centers from the hundreds of millions of farmers moving from the farm to the city. We should worry even more about those left on the farm. Can they feed the ones that leave? No farmers, no food.

Throughout history, rice has brought down regimes and caused wars across Asia, while the West has so far remained unaffected and disinterested in rice. Now Asia is joined at the hip to Western economies. If rice shakes China, the whole world economy will tremble. Rice is not just about how much is grown, but even more about who grows it and the way it is marketed and who buys and sells the farmland that grows the rice.

A mass rural migration is under way in China, one without precedent in history. In the next 15 years, perhaps more than 250 million souls will leave family farms and move into the cities. As the population shifts from farm to city, the challenge will not merely be how to receive all the poor rice farmers into the city and provide education and other social services for them. It will also concern how to efficiently produce, market, and sell the rice they left behind.

This is a bigger story than China; it is primarily about the social and agricultural upheaval arising from such migrations across Asia.

Impoverished farmers lack the financial ability to respond to market and technological changes while feeding the hundreds of millions in the nearby cities. In urban China alone, we are talking about perhaps 1 billion people living the urban life by 2030. As urbanization in China expands in its 12th five-year plan (2011-2015), the rural rice farmer could be left out financially as others grab the profit from the fluctuations in the price of his rice and the value of the land that he farms.

There are dark, foreboding shadows of tension between increasingly poor and hungry people inside the cities and farmers who barely can subsist on what is grown in the countryside. Unless the farmers become businesspersons, earn title to the real property assets they manage, and have enough to educate their children who leave the farm, Asia may tumble into social and agricultural chaos.

As the world rice price has become more and more confused since 2008, Stephen Jones, Managing Director of Live Rice Index once said to me, "There must be a better way, Milo." That phrase of his haunted me as I wrote this book. Perhaps this book is a path to that "better way." I would call it the turning of the rice market into a kind of world wheat market, with good price discovery and transparency and forward pricing for both the buyer and the seller.

Surely, there is a path to a better way through all the obstacles of the Asian rice culture. To succeed, China and other Asian rice nations must face the challenge of those who remain on the farms as well as those who leave for the cities with a bus ticket, a little cash in their pockets, and scant education.

The stakes are high. Five hundred years ago, India and China were the largest bases of wealth in the world, but that wealth was stuck in place. Now the ownership and farm management of that vast wealth is in motion. The local rice industries in Asia still are a sleepy, backward market in comparison to Western, buoyant, transparent markets, such as energy, metals, soybeans, wheat, and other grains.

In Asia today, two cultures clash on rice pricing. India is suppressing the price as well as it can to feed its poor cheaply, while China has methodically pushed up its rice price support to nearly twice the Indian price to keep people farming it. In the last two decades, to its credit, China has dramatically reduced the number of abjectly poor in its country.

The implications of current rice pricing schemes are global. Large swings in surplus and deficit could destabilize farm profits and prices for urban consumers. It is not about the price of rice but its ability to move in a market that is open and responsive to the global economy. There must be a freer, market-oriented way for rice.

I would like to reach anyone who wants to understand the importance of rice in Asia, who can conceive of the rice industry modernizing in the next decade, and who would like to know how what is going on in Asia could eventually affect their portfolio and wealth.

I would also like to reach rice farmers who are interested in becoming successful entrepreneurs, and I want to reach the firms that service farmers, that buy from farmers, the firms that process rice, and the firms that price rice internationally. Rice must transform itself from a way of life and an ancient culture, many thousands of years old, into a marketed commodity that is using a great deal of the world's most precious of resources: water.

Napoleon Bonaparte is rumored to have said: "Let China sleep, for when she wakes, she will shake the world." It has also been said that "as rice goes, so goes Asia." The rice markets are awakening. The reverberations begin.

ABOUT THE AUTHOR

"The precious things are not pearls and jade,
but the five grains, of which rice is first."
—CHINESE PROVERB

Milo Hamilton is senior agricultural economist and co-founder with Kevin Ries of Firstgrain.com, a service that advises others on markets. Firstgrain.com seeks to turn its customers into a rice market force with an edge, level the playing field for rice farmers to help them prosper and to respect each other as professionals.

For the last 13 years, his staff has been watching the rice markets across the globe and works with customers who desire that assistance. For the last three decades, Mr. Hamilton has been instrumental in the birth and development of the CME Group rice futures contract in Chicago and has used it extensively in various hedging strategies for his current customers. He has served on the boards of many rice associations, advises customers throughout the global rice marketing chain, and is senior editor of the weekly publication, the *Firstgrain Rice Market Strategist.*

Mr. Hamilton is a global authority on rice, and world wire services regularly quote his ideas. He has been involved in the rice markets for 32 years. He has written many articles for various agricultural publications and is a speaker at conferences throughout Asia and the Americas. Mr. Hamilton has an English Literature degree from Stanford University in Palo Alto, California, and agricultural economic degrees from the Universities of Missouri and Minnesota. From 1976 to 1981, as a journalist, speaker, and book author at Professional Farmers of America, Mr. Hamilton trained buyers, merchants, and farmers in the skills of risk management and hedging.

For 18 years, Mr. Hamilton managed rice procurement and risk management for Uncle Ben's, Inc., a Mars Incorporated company. In that capacity, he sourced rice and traveled throughout the rice markets of Europe, Asia, and the Americas.

Milo Hamilton lives in Austin, Texas with his wife, Jan, and his little Pomeranian, Penney. He is surrounded by his children and their families.

SHADOWS YET TO COME

R ice is a story about East and West. There is an old saying from the Bible (Psalm 103:12) "as far as the East is from the West." That is no longer necessarily the case. East and West are starting to come together now. It is inevitable. For those who want a deeper understanding of how that is happening and how that will change the world, read on. And to those in the know, the key to Asia is rice.

We face two visions of the future: one of despair and death, or one of hope and prosperity. Likewise, there are two scenarios for Asia's future, and indeed, the future of millions of people is at stake.

A VISION OF DESPAIR, A VISION OF HOPE

As we confront the momentous social changes coming to Asia, humanity holds the power to turn despair into hope. Much of that power lies in the mindset of those who guide market development and farm support programs. The mindset of many is that those farmers left to farm in the years ahead will remain in debt, in the dark, uneducated, and incapable of managing wealth. In fact, the farmer could face virtual extinction, and when we are without farmers, we are without food.

What those farmers need is not a regime to keep prices low or high. They need the ability to run their farms like a business, attuned to the acreage they grow, and attuned to the markets as the flow of information and technology accelerates and the values of global commodities shift continually up and down.

As providers of food, twenty-first-century farmers need the freedom to grow what makes them money, what the supermarkets and restaurants are telling them to grow. Governments need to give them that freedom and stop rigging their rice price.

Even today, a huge migration has begun from the rice fields to the cities. What will become of those who leave, and of those who remain on the farms? In short, those who leave must obtain the money, education, and skills to take up new disciplines. And those who remain on the farm must become savvy business people who are prosperous enough to feed the cities. That will require the full array of farm credit, technology, market price discovery, and communications that now exist or have not yet even been invented. The farmer will need those tools to manage the weather and markets, deal with climate change, and grow rice in sufficient abundance. The agriculture and open grain markets of Arkansas, the delivery area for American rice futures, needs to migrate its way of doing grain business to the vast rice fields of Asia. There is no other way to a better future for all.

We have the potential for prosperity. We also face the potential of very low rural incomes if the feudal agricultural system continues, centrally controlled and top down, with uneducated and disconnected farmers. In time, they will be unable to meet demand. With poor communication and lack of entrepreneurial initiative, the distribution channels will clog up and continue to show major storage losses. The countryside will be unable to feed the cities. The result: urban hunger, rural poverty. This situation will destabilize Asia and thereby the world.

This, then, is the story of the world rice market and its farmers that have farmed rice in China for many thousands of years. It is also about the massive change that must come to the world in the next 15 years, in the blink of an eye. It is the tale of how the rice price was discovered for eons, how it has been established for the last 40–60 years and where the rice market could hopefully end up in the next two decades.

How does the future look in, say, 2030? If one scenario is despair and the other is prosperity, what will be the nature of things yet to come? What would Father Time want to show us about our lives then?

IF OUR PATH REMAINS UNALTERED ...

If the mindset of farm programs maintains the status quo, I see Asian farmers becoming increasingly destitute. I see small tenured operations in which uneducated laborers lack the income and an understanding of marketing and money management. They will remain peasants or part-time workers, unable to respond to the demands of modern food markets, with a decreasing supply of available land and the water so crucial to the crop. They will be wards of the state, not businesspersons.

Though nations dream of self-sufficiency in rice, they cannot have that without self-sufficiency in unpolluted water supply and toxic-free land plus adequate logistics. Self-sufficiency cannot come as an extension of a feudal agricultural system of small land-tenured plots run by farmers who are outside the technological and educational loop of the rest of the world. Whether a nation keeps prices low or high, it will lose that coveted self-sufficiency. As a result, people must eat less and starve, or else import rice or buy grain hectares abroad to fill the gap.

Migration from Asian farms is inevitable. It stands to be the largest and swiftest mass migration in human history.

As a point of comparison, the migration of African Americans from the rural south to other regions in the USA has been estimated from 1910 through 1970 as less than 7 million persons. In China, the scale of the mass migration that lies ahead is nearly unimaginable. Moreover, unlike the U.S. migration, it is a planned migration.

Such a migration, of course, comes with huge social change. Governments may want to slow down or speed up that migration. Without enough jobs in the city to go around, unemployment may swell amid social turmoil. Some farm programs, therefore, are designed to keep people on the farm as long as possible. "Self-sufficiency" is really a code word in some cases for keeping people down on the farm.

In 2012, about half the Asian population was rural. In 35 years, according to projections, it could be 15 percent or less. It could be more than that, or less, but we could soon be seeing at least a 20 to 30 percent decline in rural populations in the two largest countries in the world, India and China. Of the 2-plus billion people in these two countries, we are talking about a migration of several hundred million. The historical urbanization in the West pales in comparison.

It is already clear that China and India now watch each other closely. China has been a leader in the East in freeing up society to do business in the cities. When China changed, the Soviet Union began to change. Now China must lead the transformation of farming into a business venture, in which the farmer profits and the farmer can buy and sell directly to consumers of rice. In addition, the farmer should have some ownership of the land he tills. Farmland should follow the cities and be privatized to create wealth. This outcome will challenge China's basic beliefs about agriculture and the collective and land ownership. As China awakens its rural sector to privatization, Asia will change. As Asia changes, the world will change. Napoleon was right, but it is the rice farmer who must awake first and shake China and then the world. Rice through China could shake the world.

India and China are urbanizing; the cities are receiving people from the farms. Currently, people are finding the work and the rewards much better in the cities, and so they will continue to migrate. They don't miss the hard work and indentured poverty on the farms.

People will go to where the jobs are. When profits and prosperity decline in the rural areas, people go elsewhere to find employment and opportunity. This has happened in the West, and it's now happening in Asia. Once relocated to the city, the farmers are often viewed as unable to take care of themselves. They are not seen as business managers, after all, and so they are considered incapable and largely not trainable. They will be looked upon, basically, as displaced serfs, poor feudal peasants without land or wealth, who now must live off the state. Unable to become business managers, they will despair, becoming impoverished and unemployed.

As the exodus accelerates in the decades ahead and things remain unchanged, farmers may increasingly slip in productivity. The rural sector could become a farm museum of tiny land plots, fixed in time. China could become a Japan on a gigantic scale. Landless migrants will increasingly demand that the state take care of them. As optimism wanes that rural areas can provide the hope of prosperity, farms will start to be abandoned. As the farmers grow old, no one will want to replace them.

Those who remain on the farm will be unable to make enough food. They will age, with their sons and daughters long gone. A whole generation of farmers is being lost for lack of mentoring. Agricultural enterprise requires the passing on of skills, generation to generation. The learned skills of farming over many years are in danger of disappearing.

A BRIGHTER SCENARIO

The solution lies in altering this status quo mindset and developing a new and hopeful vision. Imagine a world in which rice prices move the way that wheat prices do, internationally, with forward markets, with the benefits of price discovery, and transparency throughout the marketing chain. There would then be one world rice price, not many, as it currently the case. There would be one price, with discounts and premiums for location and quality. The prices would flow freely and without borders like the rains and rivers, which provide the water to grow the rice.

Asia and the rest of agricultural world are at a crossroads.

Is the farmer a prosperous supplier who can manage money and deliver product to a food marketing chain successfully and efficiently, without large losses? Will he connect freely with the markets, pricing his crop locally, relative to supply and demand? Will he be able to change what he grows rapidly in tandem with market conditions? The answer could be yes, but the top-down market management that is common in the Asian rice industry first must change.

Farm management, instead, has to be from the bottom up, not dictated from above with prices set out of some central command center. It has to be from the man or woman in the field who can hire and fire people, doing the business of farming and producing the stuff. No other farm market is quite like the rice market in which the prices are set firmly from the top down. Such a system gives farmers an unclear or stale price signal.

As a sophisticated businessperson, the farmer will take advantage of technology, using local forward markets to price his rice. He will be linked in on a global scale to markets throughout the world that are involved in pricing his commodity. He will be receiving weather information and price information over a smartphone or an iPad on his farm. He will be able to respond as conditions change, in a way that makes sense. He'll have a clear view of the market, straight through his marketing chain to the consumer. Money will be made in the transparent, digital light, not the dark. He will have enough money to buy a digital book, learn new ways to farm and make social connections on the Internet.

In the United States today, just about 2 percent of the population work directly on the farms, but 46 million people—about 14 percent of the population—receive food stamps. The U.S. food stamp program, estimated at $80 billion per year in transfer payments, goes directly to the wallets of the people who need the subsidy so that they might eat better. Such should be the system in Asia. Cash goes to the farmer, who feeds us, and cash goes to the poor who cannot afford high grain prices. And as for grain prices, let them freely trade.

The unintentional waste in the less developed world is in the logistics of moving food from the field to the cities. By contrast, in highly developed and highly prosperous environments, the waste is intentional and tied to people's tastes. Up to 30 percent of all vegetables in the UK are thrown down in the field and never used because of urban dweller's demands for quality. Rightly or wrongly, waste in the West is by choice, not by chance and poor logistics.

As the cost of water increases, we will have to find new ways of dealing with the food and water situation. One way could be to actually move some farming into the cities. As long as water is given away nearly for free, you don't worry about the waste of food. Water and food are joined at the hip.

There is a pessimistic mindset of many in Asia that the farmer lacks the education and resources to ever succeed as a farm manager without top-down controls on the price he receives and the land he farms.

In its current incarnation in Asia, the state-mandated rice prices give us no assurance that rice farmers will attract the means to adapt to the changing needs of urban populations. Asia should consider a slightly different mindset. A vision of despair could become one of hope and prosperity.

WHY I CARE SO MUCH ABOUT RICE

When I told my rice friends I was writing something on rice, they asked, "What is it about? Why are you writing it?" I have written down what I know about rice for one simple reason: some of those who know about rice are not telling and those who tell do not know.

I do not know everything about rice; no one knows everything about anything. But I know more than many who write about rice. Rice is more than statistics on a piece of paper. It is an ancient Asian culture that is many thousands of years in the making. Rice was, most likely, discovered and first cultivated in China.

In the end, I want to share my love for rice and the farmers who grow it and for those who mill, store, and sell the finished product. I want to share with you what I have learned from three decades in the rice marketing chain, a mere nanosecond in the history of rice. Rice is a humbling subject to undertake. The grain is small but its impact is monolithic on the history of humanity.

I have helped build rice markets. I have started rice businesses. I have traded rice for profits and risk control. Now I advise CEOs of major rice concerns, as well as governments, regulators, and exchanges.

You do not have to know how to spell the word *rice* or *rice farmer* to be concerned about the fate of rice and its role in world markets. And you should be concerned, very concerned.

I do not make many forecasts about the price of rice or the rice industry here, although that is my profession as an agricultural economist.

I will make one prediction, and that is that Asian agriculture, long underfinanced and overlooked by the money people in the world's capitals, will come into its own in the next decade and the rest of the twenty-first century. It is the great overlooked opportunity in Asia.

Agriculture is largely an untapped opportunity in Asia for digital services. I focus on the marketing side of rice farming, but that is only the tip of the digital "rice berg." On the far side of the Pacific from the USA is a blue ocean of untapped possibilities, new networks and trade associations among farmers, as well as the technological specter of urban farming as water costs and food safety concerns escalate.

Agriculture is largely physical in Asia and indeed elsewhere now, not yet very virtual or digital, but all that must change. Farming must change from feudal to virtual in the years ahead. Individuals cannot set rice policy but they can provide services to lighten the farmer's load. Power must come to the rural sector. In the case of India, for example, solar power may not be changing heavy industry, but it is bringing digital light to rural communities that have shut down in the dark in the past and can now stay open during the night. A well-charged iPad and a solar-powered overhead light can transform the rural world. China is working on solar power systems that would be self-sustaining and profitable by 2020.

Like travel, real estate, publishing, banking, medicine, and entertainment, the power of technologies and the World Wide Web will transform all the rice farms of Asia and all the 3 billion people eating rice from those millions of farms.

I challenge each reader to ask questions about how he or she can make a better living and live a more fulfilling life by helping rice farmers in Asia make a better living in the digital light.

Darkness has no speed and holds up transformative change. Light speeds us toward the digital future, now benefiting about half the earth and its peoples. Rice still lives on the dark side of our digital planet.

Once again, rice moves nations. It brings down regimes. It feeds 3 billion people, and yet it is produced on a total acreage about the size of France. It's the largest single employer in the world, bigger than Wal-Mart or the entire U.S. government.

The world's largest rice producer, by far, is China. Next largest is India, and then Indonesia and Bangladesh. By contrast, the United States produces less than 2 percent of the world's rice but ships 9 percent of world's rice trade. Half its rice is sent abroad. The U.S. grain markets feed the world, and all that has been learned from U.S. grain markets has made its way into the tiny U.S. rice market and the farmers that grow it. I have travelled extensively in Asia, but the U.S. rice market is my backyard. In the USA, rice is a crop grown to generate money, not feed the family. Rice in the West is largely a cash crop; in Asia, it is largely a subsistence crop and still a way of life.

China not only is the world's largest rice producer, but it also is the largest rice consumer. It is by far the largest food market in the world. Its food demand continues to outpace its domestic production, creating a market opportunity for exporting countries, such as the United States. In 2012, it was the top export destination for U.S. agricultural products at $26 billion, up from a mere $2.1 billion in 2002. The pending acquisition by the Hong Kong-based Shuanghui International Holdings, Ltd. of Smithfield Foods, Inc., the largest U.S. pork producer, shows the desire to not merely buy food from the West but also to acquire the marketing and quality-assurance skills of the West for the benefit of Chinese citizens.

The pork industry also began in China millennia ago, when some hungry person ate some unfortunate hog that roasted in a fire. So the story goes. China is still today a pork and rice culture, and that culture has spread across the Pacific Rim and its islands, just as the wheat culture moved out from the Mesopotamian Valley, both east and west therefrom. Through the pork market, China has become a major player in the corn market. In India, it is the humble chicken that is changing diets there, and grain consumption.

Rice represents nearly half the food expense of the poorest people in the developing world, and 20 percent of total household spending goes to rice, according to the International Rice Research Institute (IRRI). U.S. households spend only 6 percent of their incomes on groceries, a report from Euromonitor International indicates. Many of Asia's poor try to survive on an income of less than two dollars a day. They lack food, clothing, and shelter. If the price of food, principally rice, rises, then they immediately have less money for other purposes.

Somehow, the price of rice and the availability of rice must be separated for these Asian poor and separated as well from the marketing needs of the rice farmer.

PART
GROUND
ZERO:
RICE AND WATER,
JOINED AT THE HIP

"[Water shortages] threaten the very survival of the Chinese nation."
—WEN JIABAO, FORMER CHINA PRIME MINISTER, AS QUOTED IN *THE ECONOMIST*.

My rice customers, particularly farmers, are not in the rice business. I tell them they are in the water conversion business, converting groundwater and rainfall into rice starch. As the nations of Asia strive to increase rice production, they must escalate water consumption.

China faces extreme water problems with uneven distribution between the north and the south. According to *The Economist* recently, severe water stress is defined as access to less than 1,000 cubic meters of water per person per year. China's average is 450 cubic meters.

About 80 percent of its water is located in the south, while half the population and two-thirds of the agricultural production is located in the north. In Beijing, people have just 100 cubic meters of water per person per year. The water table there has plunged by 300 meters in the last 20 years. Pollution is accelerating this shortage condition and bringing it to a head. Only about half the water in urban areas is fit to drink.

We believe that the rice-growing area of Asia may be nearing a peak, and water problems are growing worse each year. In the last decade, harvested rice area has increased about 6 percent. Such a pace will be hard to replicate in the next decade, at least in Asia. Meanwhile, rice consumption has increased 19 percent in the last decade. Under the current systems of production and technology, Asia is nearing the end of its ability to increase the area under production.

Increasing yield while sending farmers to the cities, maintaining food and water safety, meeting the uncertainties of climate change, avoiding the use of GMO rice, and holding constant the level of aquifers puts nearly impossible requirements on global rice production in the decade ahead. The emphasis in the world press is on rice production rising to record levels, but the world press fails to mention that rice demand is also rising. In China and India, despite their massive rice stocks, the ratio of stocks to use is stagnant. What if expanded social welfare programs in those countries further stimulate food grain consumption for the very poor by some very large multiple?

The rice crop is utterly dependent on water supply, from the sky and from aquifers. Rivers flow between nations. Rice is also a commodity whose water source flows between nations, somewhat beyond sovereignty. On a use basis, world rice stocks, though adequate currently, seem to have flattened out or are starting to decline again.

Meanwhile, food demand could increase somewhat among the abjectly poor. Recently, India has embarked on a Food Security Bill to increase the supply of very cheap food grains to more than 800 million of its poor. The future of rice demand in Asia is in flux. Grain markets are not just about producing more; they are also about efficiently handling the storage and logistics of rice. Today, when monsoons come to India, massive stocks are left to spoil in the rain.

At present, about 53 percent of China is urban, but only 35 percent of its urban population possesses an urban residency permit, or *Hukou*. That is the document that permits a person to register for such things as pensions or local schools, or to qualify for local medical programs. If the federal government steps in to help out, up to 70 percent of the population could gain full urban welfare benefits by 2025. That might unleash a huge amount of domestic demand.

Markets are not just about food security; they are also about food safety. The tragic death of 23 children in India in July 2013 shows there is more to a school lunch program than excess grain stocks given away at a fraction of their market cost.

Governments can control grain, but they cannot completely control water. They can control rice prices and to whom rice is distributed, but Mother Nature distributes the water and it comes from the sky, rivers, and the aquifers.

Those aquifers are on the decline in parts of Asia, as they are in parts of the United States. The Chinese understand water shortages and can act on them with more coordination than can any other large country in Asia, but they also, understandably, are afraid of facing the conflict that water rationing entails. It takes a large and increasing population to create a water shortage, but India and China face water shortages, and it's not getting much better.

To manage the water, the United States alone will need to put a lot of money behind it. Estimates run as high as $416 billion to deal with leaky water lines and contamination by 2020. Between 2000 and 2008, levels in aquifers, the underground storage areas used by agriculture, dropped at a rate three times greater than at any time in the previous century.

The rate of rice production growth in Asia, so highly dependent on water supplies, will require significant water management. Rice uses more than twice as much water as does wheat. It needs the rainfall, the flooding rivers, and the groundwater.

"The tiger is not held in by the bars but by the space between the bars."
—ZEN PROVERB

Zen philosophy, in my limited understanding of it, focuses our mindset on things overlooked. In the Zen worldview, the obstacles we face are, in fact, the way through problems. Obstacles exist in the way rice currently prices itself through the marketing chain. The tiger, for example, is not restrained by the bars on the cage but by the spaces between the bars. The tiger in the rice market is water.

"When you boil your rice, know that the water is your life."
—ZEN PROVERB

Likewise, when you boil your rice, as this proverb is saying, understand that the essence of your existence is in the water that you are using to grow and to prepare your rice to eat. The rice market is a world shaker and is now an Asian economic tiger we barely hold by its tail.

Rice remains a marvelous food. Rice is the ultimate convenience food and is eaten largely as it arrives in an African port, milled and in a bag. It is a concentrated or virtual form of water import. We literally eat most of the water that we consume every day, according to a recent finding of the International Mechanical Engineers Association—92 percent to be exact. Food is a code word for water consumption by humans.

The majority of our water is used for agriculture, and China maintains some control over the waters of much of South Asia because it controls the source of many Asian rivers, and because the mountains of Tibet, which it controls, are essentially the "water towers" of Asia. Rice is grown from rivers in India, Pakistan, and Southeast Asia, and those rivers flow from the ice that melts in the mountains above them. The one who owns the mountains sets the rules of melting ice and rice.

Clearly, water matters. And it has throughout history. In the north, in ancient times, rice was by far the most expensive grain because water was even scarcer then, particularly in North China, and rice needs water. These days, rice is grown largely in flat regions near great rivers. Of the total groundwater used, the majority (perhaps as much as 70 percent in China) still goes to the growing of rice.

In Asia, rice and water are inseparable. To deal with growing populations, with their increasing urbanization, rising income, and concerns over food safety, the nations of Asia must deal with the water issue. In my mind, the only way you can deal with the problem of insufficient water is to stop trying to be self-sufficient in what is grown. That is a big change for Asia, which has made self-sufficiency in food grains a number-one priority, next to its military strength.

Once you don't have enough water, you can't be self-sufficient in food. You have three choices: Tell people to leave, start importing boatloads of water, or turn to "virtual water," which is a term developed by Canadian agricultural economists and of which Beijing is very much aware.

You virtually buy water by importing grains and meats from suppliers or sourcing it from plantations you own in other countries. You go to the world market to cover your lack of water self-sufficiency. When you import a Smithfield country ham, you are importing the water used to grow the corn to feed the hogs that made those hams and you are guaranteeing to the Chinese consumer the U.S. pork is safe to eat.

So far, China has given up self-sufficiency in animal feed but hangs onto it in food grains. If there is a shortage of feed, you can slaughter animals. If there is a shortage of food grains, your citizens go hungry. That, at least, is the mindset in Asia. A different and pro-trade mindset is to keep world food grain trade growing, so it can serve as virtual rice stocks when needed. Obsessing on self-sufficiency starves world grain trade, so rice is not there when you need it. As a rice buyer for 18 years, I encouraged buying competition because that meant more rice to choose from when I needed it, and I bought many millions of metric tons of paddy rice. I welcomed other buyers into my market with open arms. More buyers mean more rice; it is about that simple, but countries simply care about what sells to the voters. The sole strategy of most politicians is primarily to get re-elected. Self-sufficiency is an easy sell to voters in almost every country.

The safety of meats and milk and now rice is a very big deal in China, which until recently had focused more on food security at the expense of food safety. Take your eye off the food safety tiger to build rice production and it may eat you. China has farmers that, reportedly, will not even eat what they grow. I have never met such a rice farmer in my 32 years of traveling the globe to buy rice and other ingredients. If true, it is a sad state of affairs.

Once, China had 100 percent self-sufficiency in food and feed grains, and it was a small exporter of soybeans, which, as is the case for rice, it discovered thousands of years ago. Now, it buys 60 percent of the world's soybeans, and imported soybeans are about 12 percent of its total current water needs, according to recent calculations. Each percentage point of food and feed self-sufficiency lost for China shakes the world grain markets. It has been importing its water, via the import of soybeans, and that has shaken world oilseeds markets from Iowa to Brazil.

China also discovered rice and in 2013 most likely will be the largest rice importer. Could it end up buying more rice internationally in the years ahead of us? It is not who invents something, but who has the water to grow it and who wins the rice business.

I'm not a water expert, but I know a bit about rice markets. And I know that a linchpin in the rice issue is that it is so closely tied to water. At the bottom of the rice problem within countries and what holds back trading is the perception that something must be done about water.

Water is unequally distributed in Asia, as elsewhere in the world. Some areas of South Asia have plenty of water, delivered by the monsoon rains. Indonesia and Malaysia and the Philippines have enough water—and plenty of typhoons. These nations have little per capita problem with water, yet it is very expensive to grow rice there because of all the islands within their borders. A U.S. Department of Agriculture (USDA) study concluded that the island nations in Asia might never be capable of feeding themselves as the years pass, although they aspire passionately to rice self-sufficiency.

There also is plenty of water in Thailand, Vietnam, Laos, Cambodia, and Myanmar. Myanmar and Thailand have great potential to export rice because they, more or less, control their rivers. Thailand controls the entire Chao Phraya River, from its headwaters in the Bhumibol and Sirikit dams, all the way down to the Gulf of Siam. That's why for a thousand years it has been able to export agricultural commodities without disruption. A lot of it has to do with the magnificent waters that Thailand owns. It's sort of a micro version of the United States, which has the headwaters of the Mississippi within its control. Other regions, such as Europe and Africa, have to slice up ownership of rivers with their neighbors.

THE RIGHTS TO THE RIVERS

The crux of the controversy is the riparian rights of people to the flow of rivers. Who owns the water in those rivers? Is it the people above the dams, or below the dams? Is it the people of Austin, Texas, or is it the people of El Campo, Texas? Who owns the water that comes out of the Mansfield Dam on the Colorado River about 10 minutes from my home? Who owns the hydroelectric power in the dam? Where does that energy go? These are unresolved questions in Texas under one government and one legal system. In Asia, where many countries barely coexist, those thorny questions are their very life and wealth.

What happens to a region when a drought lasts for years? That is simply not a question in monsoonal Asia. Multiyear droughts, however, are a fear in the Southwestern USA and also in places such as Northern Africa. Droughts there have lasted for more than a decade, causing mass migration and the collapse of native societies.

It's not just rice but also the water that produces the rice that will be the source of a lot of social difficulties in the next few decades. I'm hopeful that countries can work together, but first they need to admit the problems. That can be difficult because, for ages, there was enough water for everybody. That is changing.

China has 1.3 billion people, over 20 percent of the world's population. Yet, it has only 7 percent of the arable land and 7 percent of the fresh water resources. Rice is largely the reason that it takes China 5 to 20 times more units of water per GDP unit than in the industrialized West. It's the big sucking straw in the aquifers of East and South Asia. China uses 20 percent of its renewable freshwater resources every year. India uses 34 percent of its water resources. By comparison, Brazil, the Russian Federation, Laos, Cambodia, and Myanmar use less than 3 percent of their water resources.

Guess who will still be exporting rice in 20 years? You guess right; these countries endowed with lots of water. Someday, rice will flow from countries that have the water to those that lack the water. It is about that simple. The USA uses 16 percent of its renewable water resources annually, and Thailand, 13 percent. These big rice exporters are less water endowed than are most of their competition and even major customers such as Nigeria, which withdraws less than 5 percent of its water resources each year.

Water is the Achilles heel of China, which is rapidly becoming the largest economy in the world and acquiring material assets rapidly across the wide earth. India is worse off in terms of water resources than is China and its population is growing faster.

Chinese food buying can change the fundamentals of food markets in short order. For example, China buys peanuts from India, but in 2013, a shortage of Indian groundnuts, one of which is peanuts, caused China to buy half the peanut stocks in the USA in a brief period of time. This action was unexpected, although China already imports the lion's share of its walnuts, pecans, and almonds from the USA.

India and China have some points of conflict at their borders. China has the ability to divert water going to South and East Asia and use it for dams to irrigate Chinese land and hydroelectric projects. This is a fact of history. China has acquired control over the headwaters of certain rivers because it controls Tibet and its mountain glaciers.

According to *The Economist*, China wants 15 percent of its power consumption to come from clean, renewable resources by 2020, up from 9 percent currently. This shift in power consumption is driving new dam building inside China. Some of these new dams are on rivers that debouche into Southeast Asian countries, several of which are major rice exporters.

Tibet is not a barren wasteland. It is a place of ice. Its ice eventually melts and pours out into the humid plains of the Indus, the Ganges, and the Mekong, to name a few rivers. There's very serious concern that, as China builds more dams, the flow of those waters could decline. Moreover, glaciers grow when snows exceed the annual melt. They retreat when the melt is greater than the snowfalls. Climate change can also affect the rate of river flow over time.

THE DAY THE RIVER STOPPED

"In 1995, Laos, Thailand, Cambodia and Vietnam established the Mekong River Commission to assist in the management and coordinated use of the Mekong's resources. In 1996, China and Burma (Myanmar) became 'dialogue partners' of the MRC, and the six countries now work together within a cooperative framework."

—WIKIPEDIA

The flow of the Mekong River can be temporarily diminished, based on what China wants to do with dams on that mighty river on any particular day. Many years ago, the *Far Eastern Economic Review* reported that Thailand helped move toward a river management agreement among countries along the Mekong River: Laos, Cambodia, Vietnam, and Thailand. However, neither Myanmar nor China, which were supposed to join, originally agreed to participate.

So the story goes, the four signatories tried to promote the idea anyway by crossing the Mekong in a ceremonial barge. About half way across, the barge was grounded, because the river level went down. A cable from Beijing was sent that said, in so many words, "We were so sorry that your barge was grounded but, the fact is, we had to fill a dam that day. We would point out that we did not sign any agreement, neither ourselves nor Myanmar."

China told those countries along the Mekong that no agreement would happen without their involvement. The point was taken. The Mekong River is critical to Cambodia and Vietnam as well as to Laos and Thailand, all exporters of rice. The Mekong River is very big and holds more fish than all the lakes of the EU. China has established itself as a key player in any water agreements in South Asia. Because it controls Tibet, it controls the headwaters of several major rivers that debouche through South Asia and Southeast Asia, an area that comprise 22 countries, some contiguous to China.

The one that owns the headwaters of rivers owns the gold of the twenty-first century, which is the blue gold of water. The blue gold produces the white gold, rice.

"WATER IS FOR FIGHTING OVER"

U.S. agriculture is not the only food exporter that faces major water shortage problems up ahead. India, for example, may be a large exporter of some agricultural products but its long-term destiny as a food exporter is in jeopardy because of its water problems with its aquifers.

India's use of water is rising, and it has not been able to develop an overall water plan. Its agricultural development on the eastern side of the country just may accelerate these water trends, with or without good monsoons in the years ahead. If India continues to expand its sizeable subsidy of food grain production, it will continue to drain its aquifers in certain regions.

The country's oil ministry does have a plan to raise the gas price substantially, which could alter the economic landscape for water use and the cost of lifting that water to a field. Input costs for Indian rice farmers have nowhere to go but higher.

China's use of groundwater continues to escalate, as well. As China builds out its cities in the "third tier" of cities, it may make more claims on the waters that flow from Tibet and the interior. The population of this remote region is about equivalent to the current population of the USA. A UN water study last year showed that China is starting to deal with the issue in part through the importation of grains and oilseeds.

Low as it is, China's level of per capita water self-sufficiency is still about 20 to 30 percent higher than is India's. Yet China is now on the road of importing more food, while India is on the road of exporting more food grains. Water and food policy is often driven not by natural advantage but by local politics.

Never has there been a century when water was as much of a problem as it is now. The major reason for migration today is not military conflict; it is water. People migrate to where they can get their water and grow their crops.

For the time being, water is essentially a free good, other than the cost to lift it out of the ground. Farmers are charged next to nothing for it; to do so becomes a highly politicized decision, with constituencies on both sides of the divide. In my home state of Texas, people are starting to take sides, due to a three-year drought that could last a few more years. People here like to quote Mark Twain, who purportedly said, "Whiskey is for drinking, and water is for fighting over."

GOOD-BYE TO SELF-SUFFICIENCY

China has been slowly relaxing its self-sufficiency standards, first on animal feed and now, perhaps, on food grains. Though it still may profess a dedication to rice self-sufficiency, it is buying rice from other nations: Vietnam, Cambodia, Laos, Thailand, Pakistan, and Myanmar. It may soon start buying rice from India, which in 2013 has a considerable surplus. I believe a good deal of the rice is smuggled across land borders into China and remains uncounted. In 2013, China is expected to become the world's largest rice importer. A protocol is pending approval in Beijing, which would allow China to buy rice from the USA. The main reason to buy U.S. rice would be food safety for the high-income markets in the cities. If and when it happens, it will shock a lot of people who do not understand the rice markets.

China may be reluctantly and sporadically moving toward the greater importation of rice and wheat. No one would have thought that was possible even two years ago. China now sees international markets as a supermarket for its needs. Its food pantry is no longer stocked totally from inside the country. Problems with heavy metal toxicity in soils in South China, particularly the Pearl River valley, may lead to the importation of more wheat, at the very least. Soils, water, and toxicity all jumble together in the minds of the food consumer in South China. Rightly or wrongly, medium-grain rice from North China is perceived to be cleaner. It certainly costs a lot more and has growing demand. So much for forecasts of rice demand sliding with rising incomes. About the time that economists make a forecast based on some equation, consumers prove them wrong. I know. I am one.

That is a huge change in Asia, where food grain self-sufficiency is prized and imports are viewed as a sign of failure. That mindset is still very much voiced inside Asia and is embedded into the Asian rice-pricing model. The Chinese import meat, oilseeds, grains, and rice. India has already given up its self-sufficiency in vegetable oil and lentils. It is the largest buyer in the world of vegetable oil, mostly palm oil, and imports a significant part of its needs.

Rice is a unique buy, much of which comes into China unreported and is imported overland and the rice trade statistics are faulty. Other commodities—crude, gold, grains, oil seeds, and iron ore—come from distant origins and the activity is transparent to world trade observers as these commodities land at various ports along the coast. Not so for rice imports.

The glamor of international commerce in rice is just a slice of the total rice activity. About 90 percent of all the raw rice bought and sold in the world is processed less than 50 miles from its point of production. That is because of preferences in Asia not to allow rice to move across borders in the rough, paddy, or unprocessed form that comes directly from the farmer's field.

The Chinese can buy rice not just from foreign seaports but also overland from rice-growing neighbors. They cannot buy sufficient quantities of peanuts, grains, or soybeans overland because the supplies come from very far away. They can't buy walnuts overland. They can't buy pecans or almonds overland. The only significant agricultural commodity that the Chinese can buy overland is rice. They will be buying rice from people who grow rice on rivers in Asia, and they own the headwaters of several of those rivers. Their decision to start relying on world rice imports is unprecedented. I believe that for years China has been buying large amounts of rice overland from Myanmar. None of these sales have been reported. Those who know do not tell and those who tell do not know.

China's decision to become less than self-sufficient in anything will shake the world of grain markets. Rice may become the shaker of world water markets.

AN AGRICULTURAL REVOLUTION

Asia faces an agricultural revolution, and it's a silent, unwilling revolution. In Asia, the fear that urban migration could leave people unemployed and starving is one reason why some governments have resisted change in the land tenure system. I believe that the change is inevitable anyway.

China faces two painful financial decisions: extending the urban social safety net to rural migrants into the cities and turning the land the farmer farms over to his charge to buy or sell or mortgage. If ex-farmers land in Chinese cities with no money from farmland sales or rental income, they become the urban poor. If they do not receive the social safety net of urban dwellers, social upheaval becomes very likely in the years ahead, instigated by these have-nots, who will remain social outcasts. The privatization of farmland inside China would be a small step that could unleash the power of the rural economy and put a little gold in farmer's pockets. Such a change of policy would put the rural areas on equal footing with the property markets in cities that are now largely privatized. This imbalance is unfair to rice farmers.

Most of Asia is suspicious of importing grains, but the countries have to feed their growing populations, and they have to deal with people of higher income who demand safer food. Poor consumers worried about food security, but now everyone, poor and better off, must worry about food safety and heavy metals in their soils and the rice they eat. The Internet in 2013 has broadcasted these food problems from the rooftops. Problems with heavy metal pollution in rice could accelerate this trend toward rice imports. A study done in the last year indicated that the number-three fear of Chinese consumers is food safety, after only inequality of income distribution and corruption. The problem is not food quantity, but toxins in their children's food. The issues of food and farmland are also joined at the hip.

This food safety issue may lead to a sea change in agriculture in the way that crops are grown and distributed. Consumers will demand to know where their food comes from. Like most real crises, it was not part of any one's food plan. Life is what happens to us as we make our deliberate food production plans. As Mike Tyson, the boxer, once said, "Everybody has a plan until they get punched in the face."

You cannot solve unsafe soils by growing more and more rice on that soil. You cannot arrest or put the farmland in jail. This is not a melamine-in-milk or rat-meat-in-sausage problem. You can send food adulterers to prison. Soils with cesium in Japan or cadmium in China are a big new problem with no pretty answers or criminals to prosecute. They are no longer a big secret, either.

Will people in Asia emigrate soon over food and air quality as well as water supplies? *The rice markets are awakening. The reverberations begin.*

From *China News*, updated May 21, 2013, 12:13 p.m. ET

Threat to Rice Fuels Latest Chinese Uproar—Guangzhou Finds High Cadmium Levels in New Scare over Contaminated Food:

Anger that authorities held on to data with potentially serious health consequences was exacerbated by the use of the state-secret argument—common throughout the government to justify refusing information requests. The tactic was even questioned by the flagship Communist Party newspaper, the *People's Daily*, on its Sina Weibo account, which called it "the magic phrase for rejecting disclosure."

Anger is also rising online that wealthy Chinese, including factory owners who contribute to pollution problems, can emigrate and raise their families elsewhere. "We should prevent Chinese people from emigrating overseas. If we did that, these companies wouldn't pollute so much," wrote one Weibo user on Monday. Users also circulated cartoon rice bowls featuring embedded skeleton heads.

Some analysts say the government refuses to release data on soil pollution in part because of fears it could unleash social instability. An accurate picture of soil pollution could endanger the livelihoods of farmers by encouraging consumer boycotts of food produced in contaminated areas. It could strengthen the voice of protesters and activists fighting to close down polluting factories, and lead to massive compensation claims by residents in areas where the soil has been poisoned by industrial waste.

China faces an immense task to feed its population as breakneck industrial development has eaten into the country's supply of arable land. An honest assessment of soil quality would put further pressure on food supplies, and challenge China's capacity to provide its people self-sufficiency, which it believes is a strategic imperative.

In response to the Guangzhou rice scandal, the *People's Daily* recently advised people to "diversify" their diets so that they weren't eating produce from just one region. That way, the degree of risk from consumption would be minimized, the paper said.

PART ONE:

TRADE ROUTE TO A BETTER FUTURE

CHAPTER 1

RICE FARMER AS BUSINESS PERSON

We must put the rice farmer first, for, without farmers, the cities will starve. In China, farmers are nice guys, they earn a mere pittance for their labor, they come in last, the last to profit from land deals, the last to know about the rice price, and the first to toil from dawn to dusk to feed the mushrooming cities. Remember, no farmers, no food.

I envision a world in which we change the way that we discover the price of rice and the way farmland trades for the benefit and profit of the farmer, not just the broker or corrupt government officials who add no value to the food chain. We need to assure the long-term wellbeing of Asia's rice farms as they shrink in number by 30 to 70 percent in the next 15 years.

In terms of farm numbers, you cannot even begin to compare the size of the Asian rice industry with the U.S. farming sector. Our sources indicate that there are between 144 to 200 million rice farms. Notice the variance around this number amounts to about 60 million rice farms. By comparison, the U.S. Department of Agriculture estimates that in the USA there are about 2.2 million farms in total with expenses of more than $100,000. Of those farms in the USA, individuals and families, not big corporations, own 85 percent. Also the U.S. farm operator is getting older. The percent of U.S. farmers 65 and older has increased almost 10 percent from 1969 to 2007, and the trend is your friend. Where do you hear about the "graying" of U.S. agriculture?

There are probably more folks on rice farms in Asia than the 313 million people living in the USA, perhaps three times as much. This gives you some idea of the scale of what I am talking about here.

The sheer magnitude of that number of rice farms—a statistic from the IRRI, which is dedicated to improving the wellbeing of poor rice farmers and consumers worldwide—can be difficult to grasp. The numerical and social scale of rice farming exceeds all other occupations. If rice farming is not a world-shaker, no profession is.

And the way that rice trades, in today's world, is this: for the most part, it does not.

Only about 8 percent of the world's total rice market is bought and sold internationally. In the few areas where it is exported, rice is a minor part of people's diet. That includes countries such as Pakistan, the United States, Paraguay, Uruguay, Argentina, and Australia. It's a short list of rice export players. Rice is a very big part of the domestic economy of other large exporters such as Egypt, Brazil, Myanmar, Laos, Cambodia, Thailand, Vietnam, China, and India. The thinness of the world rice trade is a side result of the obsessive promotion by governments of rice self-sufficiency at any cost. No other major grain aside from corn (12–15 percent of production) is so thinly traded as rice. Wheat trades 23 percent of its production and soybeans nearly 40 percent.

Rice is bought and sold in a world with a unique mindset.

When a country is wedded to rice as essential to the people's diet, the government often imposes strict controls to orchestrate the price. In 2008, when rice prices tripled, there was plenty of rice around. It was panicking governments that banned rice trading. Rice currently does not trade freely inside countries that rely upon it as subsistence crop for the population. Largely, the government mandates the price, either directly through price supports, or through input subsidies, or both. I argue that, nonetheless, such a mindset should change.

In countries where governments perceive rice to be critical to the people's welfare, the governments take control of the marketing chain. Many oppose free trading, and especially rice futures. You can see this in the demise of such rice futures markets in Thailand, India, and Japan, and the dormancy of the rice futures market in China at Zhengzhou, due to high and rigid price supports. Everyone watches the U.S. rice futures price in Chicago, but most would not trade it with a 10-foot pole.

My vision is to let the rice market trade. I see a world in which the farmer can respond to price signals and governments allow acreage to move among various commodities when possible, as occurs in the

West and to some extent in India. I see the farmer as an entrepreneur, assessing the risk and profitability of what he does, not merely just producing it for government buying agencies that let the rice spoil through neglect and poor storage.

LET THE RICE MARKET TRADE

I advocate, in other words, adopting in the East a few of the market mechanisms and approaches familiar in the West. We should adopt the kind of free and open rice markets that existed, in fact, for centuries in Thailand and Japan and around the globe before World War II.

Before the war, the rice market was open to a great degree. Governments simply lacked the money to subsidize and control prices of rice, energy, and water. Of course, in those days, most of the crops were grown with animal and human muscle power. But with the coming of the war and state control, countries in the Far East took over the control of the rice market. As national treasuries and income developed, they began using some of their resources to control the rice price to keep it affordable to the poor.

The farmer became a vassal of the state, a feudal serf, more or less. I strongly believe that nations can step back from price controls and deal with their poor rice eaters differently so that they can free the farmers to become prosperous businesspersons. In this century, if the rural population goes from 50 to 10 or 20 percent, the rice farm and the markets it sells into must change drastically. Asian rice must eventually trade like Arkansas rice, Iowa corn, or wheat from the Black Sea. Asia counts with computers now, not abaci. Yet it still has abacus-like rice price mechanisms.

An extreme example of price control was in China, where the rice price didn't change from year to year for decades. The price was mandated as a government guarantee to the rice farmer of some modest level of income. It was a hermetically sealed market, internal to itself. Its welfare state became known then as the Iron Rice Bowl. When I came into the rice market in 1981, the farm price was close to $1 per hundredweight. Now it is closer to $20 per hundredweight, a price increase of about 2,000 percent in three decades. In that same interim, gold has risen from $500 to $1,500 per ounce, an increase of 300 percent. Rice, the white gold, inside China has been gaining on gold, the yellow metal in the last three decades.

In recent years, China has been increasing the rice price support, trying to create a bit more wealth in the countryside and to keep the farmer growing rice. The goal is to maintain self-sufficiency without depending on other nations for rice, or for wheat. China does not trust the world market, especially the world rice market. Many of today's leaders knew about abject hunger back in the 1950s in a way that the West has not known for several generations. They want to be sure that they can produce what they need internally. To a large extent, it's the fundamental fear of hunger and want that steers food programs in Asia.

China's price controls create a vacuum: The world price of rice is 40 to 50 percent lower. Nevertheless, it now imports more and more rice and other grains. But whether the price rises or falls, I believe, is not the point. The point is to let the farmers determine what to grow and how to grow it, and to not orchestrate the price or what is grown and where.

If rice were allowed to trade freely, it would be the largest market in forward grain prices on this planet. Of that I am totally certain.

In Asia, rice and gold are the two favorite commodities to trade. Gold trades; it is forbidden to trade rice. I hope you are beginning to understand why. As is the case of water, rice trades the way politicians would wish all things to trade: tranquilly.

LET THE MARKET TRADE

Price supports bring more money to the farmers, but the goal of national self-sufficiency is elusive. Consider the case of Japan, which has increased its rice prices dramatically over the last few decades and yet, nonetheless, is not at all self-sufficient in food, less than 45 percent self-sufficient. You could argue that the higher the price is set, the more a country risks a loss of self-sufficiency. The farmer doesn't think about the market, and the resulting inefficiencies create problems that must be faced in the future.

Whether prices are set high or low, the intervention distorts the market. The farmer cannot become professional and business-like, which, in today's world, is what agriculture desperately needs. Even after 10 years of rising grain production, China is starting to lose control and is likely to import more and more and appears to be following in the footsteps of Japanese farm price supports. Rigid prices of $1 or $20 turn farms into food museums.

THE MAGIC OF THE GRAIN MARKETING AND MERCHANDISING CHAIN

Here is how grain markets trade in Arkansas, the largest rice-producing state in the Union.

In between the field and the city in the United States there is a merchandising business that makes money by arbitraging between the forward markets and the cash or spot markets. A lot of information is available and transparent for all to see, whether they're farmers, merchants, or large food corporations.

In the fall, when the crop comes in, the price normally falls, only to rise again when just a little of the crop is left to sell. That is the essence of the seasonality problem, which is the problem that a forward market helps to solve. It can serve as the glue to hold a market together. And that's the merchandising function that needs to be propagated and moved out into Asia and the world rice market.

To grow another 50 or 100 million metric tons of grain is not necessarily a good thing, not if it spoils from logistical inefficiencies. The infrastructure must be in place to handle a massive increase in production—that is, the storage capacity and the transportation network to move the product to the population.

You don't necessarily solve hunger by increasing production, strange as it sounds. You solve hunger by increasing production and enhancing the market structure to manage and efficiently deliver that production every day, every year. That's essential to creating a healthier grain market, as in Brazil and the United States. For example, in China in 2013, some of the 30.8 million MT of reserve corn may not be suitable for feed or processing. Stored in the kernel form, a lot of it has high moisture and is moldy. Unless someone makes money by storing grain professionally, the grain quality suffers. It takes a focused and business mindset to grow, store, and merchandise grain.

This is far from a radical concept. I'm arguing for extending the concept of grain markets that work in the West. In the last 40 years, the financial world has extended open, transparent markets to gold, to currencies, and to government debt—and they've not turned back—and more recently, to heating oil, crude oil, natural gas, iron ore, and steel. Slowly, one by one, these global markets that were supposed to be "too important to trade" are being traded.

A freer market price allows signals to flow between consumer and producer about what to provide with scarce resources in a world of climate change. We don't have unlimited water in this world to grow things. The market's signals allow the adjustments, either painful or beneficial, that are needed now based on the future that people anticipate. This is a simple concept, but the world changes more on simple and mundane ideas than on the magnificent and complex ones.

Our company, Firstgrain.com, proposed in Singapore in 2012 the creation of a world milled-rice futures contract, based on a blend of rice origins. Such a rice price index might even help form a merchandising function for strategic rice buffer stocks in Asia. The idea of buffer stocks has remained elusive even after years of discussion. No one wants to step out and do it, because there is no money in doing it. Making money is the magic that leads to action in the grain markets.

Merchants and investors could handle those buffer stocks and price them and take care of the cost of inventorying them without burden to the participating countries. A forward market, or perhaps an over-the-counter market that prices off a rice price index, could become a world price benchmark. An analogy would be Chicago wheat futures against which global wheat markets price themselves. The analogy in energy is West Texas crude, which is priced in New York City. Several markets currently have such a world price benchmark: cocoa, coffee, sugar, and soybeans, to name a few, but not rice, yet.

I visualize several local paddy or rice exchanges to price domestic rice production and a tradable rice index or over-the-counter market, perhaps located in Singapore, that prices out the indexed value of milled rice exports from Asia and perhaps the Americas.

MERCHANDISING AND PROSPERITY

The merchandising function is absolutely critical to the success of an agricultural system, but it is little appreciated or understood. It is a technical idea, like options on stocks or commodity futures. You do not get doctorates in grain merchandising; you just make money. Yet, it is the cement to a grain system that does not spoil millions of metric tons of grain every year, as is now happening both in India and China. In fact, the merchandising function is what has created a lot of the farm prosperity in the United States in the last 150 years. It's technical and dull and it requires education and marketing discipline, and it requires understanding between the government regulators, lenders, the producer, and the merchant. It is the everyday miracle that moves grain from field to grocery store in a timely and efficient manner.

In the USA, less than 10 percent of all farmers use the commodity exchanges directly, but they go to merchants who become like merchant bankers for the local farming community by arbitraging between cash and futures and moving the commodity through the distribution chain during the year. The merchant deals with the margin calls and price volatility in most cases.

When farmers get a forward market and a cash market in merchant and exchange warehouse receipts, they get a much deeper understanding of the marketplace that allows them to look at when and how they should sell their commodity. A professional farmer thinks like a grain merchandiser.

The American model is to set the poor aside and give them food through funds transfer rather than in kind, letting the farmer, the merchant, and the grain company buy and sell the market and grow what needs to be grown to fulfill the demand. It requires an education of anywhere from six months to several years to become an effective grain merchant or even a farmer who fully understands this marketing principle.

From a merchant point of view, a farmer is someone who owns a crop and must sell that crop as best he can at a profit or less of a loss during the year. Until a farmer understands that he's doing that and that there are tools available to him to merchandise that crop, so to speak, he becomes a huge gambler, or the state becomes a gambler if it fixes the price on his behalf as in China or subsidizes grain insurance premiums as in the USA.

The forward markets are basically voluntary price and crop insurance. When the possibility of profit exists, the farmer needs to seize on that and take advantage of it through a marketing plan. Chance favors the farmer who is prepared to take market action 365 days a year.

I tell my rice farmer customers to practice market gratitude. They need to be grateful for the prices they have, and the gratitude is the act of selling some of their commodity throughout the year at different times. They are able to take that marketing and decide what they plant in the coming seasons.

In California, farmers have many different crops they can produce. In parts of Asia, they can only grow rice or maybe something similar to that. Again, it gets back to what the water is worth and who will pay for that agriculture. Rice, in part, salvages land not suitable for other crops, which is part of its miracle.

What I'm advocating is not so much one particular route to agricultural success, but that every country start thinking about its farmers as people with a business opportunity. The mindset of Asian rice programs must answer the question of what the future holds. We can only watch as spectators as this story unfolds. We all must hope for a good outcome, a professional rice farmer in Asia.

RICE MARKETING BUILDS A FARM'S PROFITABILITY

What we need to do is create rice marketers out of farmer producers. In the rice-growing areas of the USA, young people just out of college understand the economics of market risk management. A farmer can't just grow a crop. He must become a rice economist. He has to know demand and supply and the relationship of his local price to the terminal price to merchandise and make a profit with his crop. He needs to locate his selling within the marketing year, just as he now focuses on micromanaging his field inputs with GPS devices and a smartphone.

I visited the home of one of my farmer customers in North Arkansas. I was admiring his beautiful home on the edge of a golf course. He said, "Milo, rice production did not buy this home; rice marketing did."

I tell every one of my farmers they should take a course in grain merchandising and think like a grain buyer, because it is the merchant and the buyer who come into the market with a plan each year. The farmer is often too emotional in his selling; he lacks a plan and fears he will sell too cheaply, and he then sells too late or too early in each crop cycle.

You need to have a plan in any financial endeavor. Any business must have a plan. Good planning does not insulate businesses from grief, pain, and bankruptcy, but it does increase the likelihood that they will succeed. Any business has to move ahead, accept new technology, and think outside the box.

Let me recommend the University of Arkansas grain merchandising courses as a way, globally, to get online education in these merchandising principles. This program is currently under the guidance of Dr. A. McKenzie, Agricultural Economist University of Arkansas, *Price Risk Management, Futures Markets*. You can find the link for this course in our appendix. It's a way that farmers worldwide and their suppliers of services can advance from a nice idea to actually getting a grain education. The course is not cheap, but you also get exactly what you pay for something. Too many expect everything for free.

Chance favors the prepared farmer who gets down to business and pays to learn how to do it right.

White Commercial (www.whitecommercial.com), a business that trains people to become grain merchandisers and a strong financial supporter of the University of Arkansas merchandising school, does want to change the way in which the world prices grains for the benefit of small rural merchant businesses and their farmers. They are my kind of people. I want to do that for rice across the globe, but they want to do it for all grains in the USA and Canada. Many of the large and international rice merchandising groups now put their new recruits through the White Commercial grain marketing courses here in the USA and at the University of Arkansas.

Online merchandising education is the single cheapest investment with the greatest payoff Asia can make to bring its domestic rice marketing chains into the twenty-first-century of agriculture.

Anyone buying or selling grain anywhere should adopt the discipline of a grain merchandiser and take the time to learn how a merchant and a grain buyer thinks and acts. A good seller appreciates how his buyer eyes the rice market. The rice buyer is his customer, and it stands to reason a good seller will understand and satisfy his customer every day.

Either you are a speculator or you are a merchant in your buying or selling activities. There is no third category of risk management in freely traded grain markets. When a farmer sells what he has grown, he needs to learn to plan his sales as a professional buyer plans his annual spend on a commodity—that is, he must focus on value and net profits. Better to take a little profit than larger losses and increased debt.

STRENGTH IN NUMBERS

I'm not saying that all farmers need to have a master's degree in agricultural economics. Small-size farm operations in Asia most likely will band together in small local networks in which they all can benefit from their shared knowledge, and let someone specialize in merchandising what is produced, hedging it, and finding markets over the Internet for that production. Cooperative marketing allows owners of small land parcels to band together for a marketing edge. I do not mean collectives and village cadres that steal the land from the farmer to profit by selling to developers. I mean voluntary trade associations to profit the farmer, not the land speculator. As Alexis de Tocqueville pointed out two centuries ago, the genius of the United States is not its big government or corporations but its small and flexible associations and groups bent on mutual benefit. He noted at the time that there was nothing equivalent to this in the Europe of his day.

Among the people in those networks will be someone savvy who understands how to price rice and how to farm the markets, so to speak, and who knows price relationships and buyers active in the region, the valley, or along the local rivers. Equipped with a smart-phone or an iPad, an individual or marketing team will be on call 24/7, trading the crop just as they do in the big grain companies. A smartphone or a tablet PC now allows an active producer or his marketing representative to carry marketing opportunities nearly anywhere he goes.

CHAPTER 2

WHY THIS MATTERS NOW

"I f there are no more farmers," says Jim Rogers, a bow-tied, motorcycle-riding investment advisor in the Far East, "we're all going to starve to death." Asia's farmers are aging, he warns, and the system of agriculture there eventually will wreak havoc. I haven't met Jim, but I've been hearing him saying a lot of the same things that I do. He pointed out recently that the USA is producing more MBA degrees than agricultural degrees. According to one estimate there were about 156,000 new MBAs in 2012 versus about 15,000 total agricultural degrees or about 10% of the total number of MBAs. Rogers asserts that those MBAs will be farming soon or driving tractors for those who do farm. I second his thinking, not just in the USA but in Asia as well.

What we need to see in Asia is a vast migration of wealth and trading savvy back to the countryside, not away from it. Politicians may not like the volatility of the commodity markets but for a farmer, they are his bread and butter. Young people have been leaving farms in droves, which is probably a necessary part of change. However, some need to remain behind or return and learn the business of farming, and pass that wisdom along to the next generation. Just as farming is moving into the cities through high technology, there should be a return of some of the younger generation from the cities back to the farm, as farming becomes more profitable. These recently educated children of farmers can help in the transformation of Asian agriculture. But there must be an incentive to return and take on the risks of farm ownerships. Peasant status will not attract the urban youth that have the education to work in the cities.

On the other hand, if wealth and talent continue to drain out of the rural sector, the logistics of food production and water management will suffer. We have seen aquifers decline and nitrogen pollution increase as food production has increased in the last half decade in the wake of the 2008 price run-up. We have also seen some quality problems develop: aflatoxin in wheat, mold in corn in North China, and heavy metal pollution in rice-growing regions in South China.

TIME IS OF THE ESSENCE

All those involved in the real business of feeding the world—the farmers, truckers, storage operators, and others—need to be rewarded year after year with opportunities to profit. If a government pumps up production without merchandising it well, the food will spoil. Mismanagement will abound, and people will continue running to the cities.

People increasingly will expect high quality, and they will demand the removal of heavy metals and anything else tainting what they and their children will eat. Water waste is an endemic problem in both the West and the East but for different reasons. Up to 25 percent of the water in China is reported to be unfit for agricultural use. Up to one-third of the length of the Yellow River, the "mother river" of China, is now too polluted for agricultural use.

As the changes come apace, time is of the essence. We must deal with those troubling water issues, and the increasing social demand for safe food; we must come to terms with climate change, soils that we cannot till, and with rapid urbanization. We must turn the torrent of new technology to our mutual advantage. For example, according to a report released in March 2013 by the Association for Unmanned Vehicle Systems International, over the next decade agriculture may account for $75.6 billion of the $82.1 billion created by unmanned aircraft systems (drones). Such activities would require a very well educated and well-financed farmer population.

THE GROWING RECOGNITION

"Milo, you are *nuts*," I often have heard, or words to that effect. "The rice market is not broken, and the Asian farmer will *never* be a businessman!" And that indeed has been a prevailing mindset throughout Asia, among intellectuals, government officials, and people at the local level. The Asian farmer, they say, simply lacks the land size and resources to behave like some 1,000-acre farmer in the United States or Brazil. Currently, there is a move in China and even now in Japan to increase the size of farms to 20 hectares (about 50 acres), which is considered a large operation. Even such a small change in farm size could lead to huge and positive benefits.

Millions of Asian farmers are indeed abjectly poor. Even though they produce the crops to feed the cities, they themselves lack the basics of food, clothing, and shelter. It's been the case for centuries and cannot change, which is a mindset of many in Asia even today. Seventy-five percent of those interviewed in Asia in one recent study said the farmer is not now to be and likely never will become a businessman. Or, we could also say that 25 percent now agree with the premise that the farmer is a businessperson. How could someone who earns less than $2 a day ever even afford any book, much less an iPad or a drone to watch his crops?

The prevailing mindset is that the business should be left to the people in between the farm and the city. However, in the chain between farmer and consumer, money is made in the dark. Those people in the middle do not want any change in that status quo, because they are making out all right and believe it is for them the best system possible. And that's a question that society itself must ask: Is there a more transparent and market-driven approach to buying and selling our food that brings the consumer and farmer closer together? The people wedged in the chain, brokers and resellers, between farm and city will never be advocates for change.

But it's already starting to happen. The large grain companies are acknowledging that information is precious and much easier to get than it was 20 or 30 years ago. At the local level, they have had to go through vast changes and layoffs and reorganization. In global commerce, information on rice markets and pricing has become more widely available. But it's not global commerce. Rather, it's the local pricing mechanisms within the borders of an Asian country that matter most to a farmer.

World trade in rice is very sophisticated, but if you drill down within the borders of some Asian countries, it's very rural, old-fashioned, and sleepy, and that's what must change. In India, the most dynamic food market is chicken production, which is on the rise, because it's a free market and diets there are changing among the youth. The Indian government has not regulated the chicken market to death. The rice market too has the potential to awaken. Inside those local borders, however, the farmer is viewed as a price taker. But, as a business manager, I believe he also can become a price-information "harvester."

When people ask me how I could possibly believe that the Asian farmer might become an entrepreneur, I feel reassured that I have gotten their attention. When they call me "nuts," they say it with energy. They are listening. They're far from bored with these ideas.

The perception that farmers should be poor is unfair. We all deserve to pursue the dream of prosperity. It's not about avarice or just making a buck. It's about the ability to dream a better future for your children, to give them an education to stay or leave the farm as they so choose. Hope is about expanding our freedoms of choice.

CHAPTER 3

THE CURRENT SYSTEM IS FAILING

A struggling restaurant that caters to the wealthy will never survive unless it has a way to gain some wealth for itself. Think of that restaurant as Asia's farming sector.

What that "restaurant" needs to become successful is an efficient and profitable operation that communicates clearly and delivers a satisfying and safe meal to the consumers, who are increasingly more affluent and demanding. Otherwise, we face a future in which indebted, bankrupt, poor farms will be trying to feed rich and thriving cities, and that's an equation that just won't add up.

Why would they stay to work on a farm when they might become, say, an accountant in the city with weekends off? If there's no extra financial benefit in farming, people will not do it. Most farmers learned from their parents about the alchemy of sun and wind and rain and water. It takes years to learn to work the land. It is a mental mindset to want to own and manage a business.

I would say this about the social and agricultural turmoil that lies ahead: There are side benefits that should accrue to Asian countries as rural populations move toward the cities by 20+ million persons per year. The history of economies in transition tells us that such demographic shifts can create wealth and may result in an added 6 to 8 percent growth on gross domestic product, a growth that lasts from five to ten decades. Such was the case with Britain in the eighteenth century and Russia, Korea, and Japan in the twentieth century. The drastic reduction in the level of extremely low-income earners inside China in the last two decades is a heartening example of this tendency toward wealth improvement. I simply say to share the wealth and give the farm to those who farm it. They bought the farm; let them own it.

THINKING OUTSIDE THE BOX

It's time to think outside the box. Even those who think the rice farmer could never be an independent businessperson have to acknowledge that some alternative outcome is preferred. In this age of direct selling and online trading sites, we now have the ability to deliver information customized and direct to each farmer and to the local marketplace. We have seen what the Internet has wrought so far. It has had profound influences on the distribution of information and market insight. The World Wide Web has changed forever the worlds of brokerage and publishing. Newspapers and magazines have felt the powerful punch of online access. The Internet's power, however, has yet to be fully felt in the realm of agriculture and food service. Amazon is experimenting with grocery delivery in Seattle. Why not deliver Amazon groceries in Chinese cities, as well?

A restaurant's patrons will not return if the service is poor and the food looks and tastes unacceptable. Asia's breadbasket needs to get much closer to the developing tastes of its patrons, and the Internet holds the promise of making that possible. You might think of that as a farmers' market on a grand scale, with the farmer able to distribute more and more to the consumers, while informing those consumers about what they are eating. The two can get together far more efficiently to nurture each other, quality food for the urban dweller, and rural money for the farmer. This is what urban farming is all about by the way: building trust between food buyer and food seller.

In this information age, you don't have to drive to the city to give your mother money. Banks need not be made of bricks and mortar; they can be virtual ones under a village tree. The ability to wire money has completely altered the model in which five brokers boost the price of, say, cucumbers by 500 percent by the time they reach New Delhi. That markup can be sidestepped. In the pessimistic view of the Indian food brokers, buying directly from the farmer dooms food brokers to joblessness. Smart brokers will land on their feet, but that is not so true for Indian cucumber farmers who need education and access to credit lines.

I'm an optimist. I believe this vision can come true. For certain, a population on the move can bring huge dividends to a society. Every time a worker moves from the farm to the city, he contributes up to six times more to the GDP than in the rural area. The rural sector has an opportunity that is unprecedented in world history. Half the global wealth could find itself in a position of mobility and change.

As the rural sector turns into a business venture, that growth in GDP might way exceed the historical rate, with both the farm and the city boosting GDP. The Internet and its delivery are shaking things up. Under the right conditions, it could be shaken up, full measure and overflowing to all the players in this food business. Think of the Internet as a global Sears's catalog, which brought urban spending to the rural famer in the USA a century ago. But more than a Sears catalog, the Internet is also a digital space where the consumer can start a business, as well. It is a space to expand consumption and small business, as well.

ASIAN ATTITUDES IN FLUX

"Some see private enterprise as a predatory target to be shot, others as a cow to be milked," Winston Churchill said, "but few are those who see it as a sturdy horse pulling the wagon."

I have tested my ideas on individuals and at rice conferences in Asia that I attended during the last decade, and the change in attitudes helped prompt me to undertake this endeavor. I never wanted to be a lonely prophet of change. I want to be on trend and on the market. That is what I do for a living.

In Saigon in 2007, when I made my point that farmers need to be transformed into entrepreneurs so that they can reap a rewarding and profitable life, an official from a large rice-consuming nation spoke up from the audience to say, "We can't do that with our rice farmers! They are just poor farmers, and we must provide for them." Later, in the cafeteria line, he told me privately, "I just want to tell you that you're right, but I couldn't say that in public. Please keep on saying and doing what you're doing. Asia needs new ideas."

In those days, I seldom got a question when I spoke. The silence was deafening and discouraged me from taking my ideas any further. Everyone seemed afraid that they would be branded as rice market heretics if they even gave the impression they were interested in such a touchy and political topic as freeing up the rice farm to become a prosperous business. Letting the farmer trade rice is like letting the farmer own and trade the land he tills. These concepts are political and intellectual dynamite to some.

A few years later, when I was invited to speak on rice in Singapore in 2010, I was astounded to discover the situation had changed radically. I could not believe I was in the same Asia as 2007. I was inundated with questions.

In 2010, I accepted the invitation to prove to myself this farm situation in Asia was totally hopeless. I expected people once again to reject my market-oriented ideas. I expected to hear, yet again, that the farmer must forever be a peasant in need of the government's care. There was a time, I admit, that I too consigned the Asian farmer to the route of abject poverty, unable to market his rice to the cities. I knew there was a better way, yet I was feeling that the attitudes were too entrenched and too ancient to change. I proved myself dead wrong about Asia. It was clear that there was tremendous interest in my ideas in 2010, just three years later.

All this change in attitude happened between 2007 and 2010. Perhaps it was tied to the onslaught of Internet access, the explosion in rice prices, or the collapse in the world economy in 2008. The interest came not just from rice merchants and economists, but also from nongovernmental organizations in Myanmar, Cambodia, and elsewhere that recognized agriculture must become a business and not in the sense of growing more stuff, but also in distributing, logistically managing, and trading and pricing that stuff for a profit.

Many people had been waiting for someone to step forward and clearly address what was on their minds. Apparently, I was not nuts in 2010. I have not spoken in Asia since that time. I often wonder if the trend continues toward market price discovery for the rice farmer.

Though the 2010 conference had signaled interest in our ideas and a dawning recognition that something must change, another Singapore gathering in March 2012 clearly indicated that much of Asia is not quite ready to act. Though many recognized the need for a global rice futures contract, issues such as delivery areas, currencies, unpredictable subsidies, and export bans among others caused many to question the currently feasibility of such contract. Our presentation at the 2012 meeting focused on the key factors that have contributed to the success of the U.S. futures contract. The content was well received by most.

The Government of Singapore asked the RSIS Centre for Non-Traditional Security (NTS) Studies to host in Singapore an Expert Working Group Meeting on Asian Rice Futures Market, which was held from March 22–23, 2012. The government knew of the interest by the International Rice Research Institute (IRRI) in such an idea and wanted to help the IRRI to be better informed by bringing together the best minds on the subject. IRRI was enthusiastic to be part of the meeting.[1]

In attendance was Dr. Ramon L. Clarete, an economist who has done research work on food security and policy, mostly in the Philippines and ASEAN. He is the Dean of the University of the Philippines School of Economics. His research endorsed our viewpoints regarding the need for increased price transparency, and our belief

---

1 | Here is the link to the actual report: http://www.rsis.edu.sg/nts/html-newsletter/report/pdf/RSIS_FutureRicePolicy_300812.pdf

that a rice futures contract could be a mechanism to help bring that about. Dr. Clarete also chairs the Rice Bowl Index advisory board.

The gathering of world rice experts was not open to the public, although the findings were published in the fall of 2012. Heads of rice agencies from all over Asia were there, including the director of the Tokyo Grain Exchange, as well as representatives from international trading houses.

The conference concluded that the proposal on rice trading faced some clear obstacles, because of the nature of rice markets inside countries in Asia. "There's nothing wrong," some traders said. "Nothing is broken." The idea was discussed at the conference, however, and we did submit a paper. We made a formal presentation, and also I wrote up a position report on what we presented that the center was kind enough to publish.[2]

The position papers represent a spectrum of views that needs to be taken into account as the world proceeds with any of the ideas that were put forth here. The bottom line of the criticism of the idea of trading rice futures in Asia is that rice is too fractionated and too differentiated into types of rice and types of markets to form a rice futures contract at this time.

Nevertheless, an informal canvass of the participants at the conference indicated that the majority was not against a rice futures contract and genuinely wanted more studies to be done to test the proposal. One idea was to run a trial of a hypothetical contract of

---

2 | You can read that paper and our presentation and others' viewpoints at: http://www.rsis.edu.sg/nts/html-newsletter/report/pdf/RSIS_FutureRicePolicy_300812.pdf

certain varieties to see what might happen to rice prices. The Tokyo Grain Exchange undertook a similar trial run before they actually launched their rice futures contract.

In summary, the Singapore exchanges were ultimately open to exploring the idea and seemed to be in a more responsive position if the rice market wants to go forward with the idea and the Monetary Authority of Singapore approves it for trading.

We pointed out in our position paper that it took 30 years to develop a small rice futures contract in the United States. Even today, in my opinion, the CME Group rice contract is a Western Hemisphere, not an international, rice market. But then the same could be said of other grain and oilseed contracts priced in Chicago. They all began as local agricultural markets in the U.S. Midwest. They grew into global platforms because of the need for forward pricing of all world crops. The Black Sea in Russia and EU wheat markets are hedged in by, or should I say priced off of, Chicago soft red winter wheat prices. That wheat is only a small portion of all the wheat grown in the USA, for example, yet it is a world price benchmark for wheat. The soft red winter wheat futures contract, for example, traded in Chicago, represents less than 2 percent of all the wheat produced in the world.

Speculators and hedge funds in Singapore, as well as elsewhere in Asia, buy and sell U.S. rice forward prices, but many fail to recognize what it really is, and a lot of money has been lost trying to rope in the U.S. price based on Asian rice values. In 2008, many from world organizations saw Chicago rice futures as the enemy of the poor around the world, singlehandedly driving world rice prices to more than $1,000 per metric ton. To me, that is totally implausible.

The big bull rice market in 2008 was due to governmental actions based largely on bureaucratic, not speculative, fear and panic. Most speculative money exited long before the price top. In the USA, foreign buyers also panicked and took the market to price extremes. Commercial buyers, not professional speculators, usually put the top in commodity price spikes. It is true for crude oil and rough rice. Buyer fear, not speculative greed, usually creates upside price extremes. But Churchill was right in his observation about views on private enterprise. It seems if all else fails, blame speculators and private businesses for our pricing woes.

In conclusion, in 2012 rice experts in Singapore generally opted to postpone our idea of starting up a milled rice futures contract. There have been, as far as I know, no further steps taken as a result of that conference.

We did get some support for our ideas, however. One supporter was the Tokyo Grain Exchange, which, not too surprisingly, was very much in favor of the idea of rice forward markets to help the rice farmer in Asia. Perhaps with changes underway in Japan, that rice futures market can again come back to life. We had the support of IRRI, and of course there was some academic interest among the economic professors at the meeting in Singapore.

But the long and short of it is that my company definitely held a minority position. I encountered many of the same objections and obstacles when we started up rough rice futures in 1981. All I can say is, "Success comes in cans and failure comes in can'ts."

There are fundamental issues and institutional obstacles concerning the rice price about which people have strong philosophies and social opinions. Nonetheless, we were not alone in saying there

might be a place for Asian rice futures. China, which was not repre-
sented at the conference, had at the time a semi-active rice contract
that was developed directly off the Chicago exchange. The Chinese
exchange studied the U.S. paddy contract in Chicago and imple-
mented it between the two rivers with physical deliveries all over the
place.

An earlier attempt at a Chinese rice contract became very active
during 1994, and it was briefly the largest volume grain contract in
the world, so the government at that time clamped down on it and it
died an unnatural death. The interest in trading rice in Asia is huge,
but the governments of Asia do not share that enthusiasm, yet.

You clamp down on a rice exchange contract by raising the
margin requirements so only commercials can take part and the
speculative part gets pushed out. I think that in the end, the grain
merchants don't care, but the government rice departments worry
about speculative enthusiasm driving the price up and creating
media havoc for them. They are against speculative involvement in
any rice market. That's the prejudice. It's extreme, I would say, in
India, which actually had a good rice futures contract before it was
shut down because the rice price went higher. Of course, Japan has
a small contract in japonica rice, but due to opposition from the
rice farmer cooperatives, it basically has gone dormant at the Tokyo
Grain Exchange.

At this time, the Zhengzhou Commodity Exchange is planning
to launch a japonica contract. China reportedly produces about 65
million MT of that type of japonica rice. It also plans to launch
a late season rice contract. Thereby, this exchange will have futures
contracts for each of the major seasonal rice crops inside China for

the north and the south. But they have a low probability of success until the rice price begins to fluctuate inside China.

WHAT WE PROPOSED

Specifically, what we proposed in Singapore in 2012 was that, first of all, futures are good for the farmers' marketplace and encourage the rational accumulation and distribution of the farmer's rice through arbitrage between cash and futures ("basis trading" is the term for this activity). They create more wealth in the rural sector, they position the farmer as a price hedger, and they lay off risk to speculators or anybody else who wants to take it on. They create a base of financing for the rural farm sector. Most importantly, from the farm to the dinner plate, they create logistics that can manage increases or decreases in production without massive spoilage. Futures that freely trade send signals as to what crops to grow each year. Farmers in the country should decide what to grow, not bureaucrats in the city. Exchanges may locate in the cities, but acreage decisions should happen in the rural areas.

We suggested that a fledgling effort be taken up—and this was included as a recommendation—to start a buffer stock in Asia, focused in Singapore, either physically there or acquired from approved warehouses, that would trade a milled rice contract of some type. There are milled rice qualities that people generally recognize as a quality standard, such as 5 percent rice. That physical amount of commodity, say half a million or a million tons, would be there for various contingencies that might occur in the region.

I pointed out in our position piece that in 2012 as much as 350,000 MT of rough rice inventory was in Chicago at any one time as warehouse receipts, not to mention the non-warehouse receipt hedge business there, probably more than one to two million MT at any one time, a major share of all the long grain rice bought and sold each year in the USA. In 2013, most of those registered receipts have been liquidated due to a shortage of supply and strong export demand. The cash price gained on futures, resulting in the distribution of exchange stocks to the trade. That is what a healthy forward market is all about: accumulating and distributing rice to the market over time.

The rice futures market in the USA actually works, despite views to the contrary. When differentials between the futures and the cash are wide, receipts accumulate. When the differentials between futures and cash are narrow or inverted, receipts disappear. It happened in wheat more than a year ago and in rice futures in 2013.

Many have talked about buffer stocks in Asia for unexpected contingencies, but few want to donate them or pay for them. One of the biggest cost of commodities is holding them as well as the flat price risk. A healthy forward market in the milled rice price could hold them, however, and that's what I suggested. If you can get a contract going in Singapore in milled rice out of Thailand, Vietnam, India, or wherever, you can encourage the local markets to build their own forward markets.

Several rice news services such as the Food and Agricultural Organization rice indexes, Live Rice Index, and Oryza.com have developed world milled-rice price series that might be a vehicle from which to develop a daily settlement price to execute on a futures exchange. The rice might also be bought and sold like an iron ore in an over-the-counter market. If the trading community trusts a rice index and its price composition and weighting, it could even be settled in currency such as U.S. dollars instead of rice, which eliminates the need for physical storage of rice. Cash or currency settlement and over-the-counter trading solves some difficult political and regulatory issues. I simply ask, "Why not take a shot?"

The world trade in rice changes hands as a processed product, which is an anomaly. Most of the world's grain and oilseed markets price out as raw, unprocessed material, such as soybeans, wheat, and corn. That is a fluke of the historical development of Asian rice markets, which I will explain later.

Singapore or some bank in Asia may have the money, the prestige, and the credibility, and I believe it could become a thought leader in derivatives, demonstrating that rice derivative contracts are okay and can be effectively used by merchants and farmers inside Asian countries.

HOW WILL RICE FARMING LOOK BY THE END OF THE TWENTY-FIRST CENTURY?

Back in 1976 when I was hired on at Professional Farmers of America, the owner and founder, Merrill Oster, who has taught me so much, said to me: "Notice the word 'professional' in our company name."

It was the driving vision of his organization, which through hundreds of seminars and newsletters and magazine articles on marketing has changed the way farmers look at the business of farming and hedging and risk management in the Midwest, the heart of the U.S. grain belt. I was involved in many of those training seminars from 1976 to 1981. I learned a great deal about how to change mindsets in agriculture. Change the mindset and feed the world. Those concepts in hedging and merchandising have now become pervasive in the U.S. rural sector for grains. Selling the grain can be as time-consuming and rewarding as growing it in the first place.

"Milo," Merrill told me, "if you farm as a way of life, it will become expensive, but if you farm as a business, it can be a very rewarding way of life." Someone is going to have to pay for the food and someone is going to have to make a profit to grow that food.

Farming is not a mindless machine of production. It's a delicate business. It's a business of interaction between the farmers and Mother Nature. Mother Nature has her own ways of doing things. The farmer has to work with her, and with Father Market, and make money. He has to make money. He needs a profit, and that profit is not a dirty word to me.

No water and clean soils, no rice, no money, no business, no farmers, no food. That's the kind of simple axiom that I see. Farmers need to have their hand in the market all year long, increasing and decreasing their market exposure as conditions during the season evolve, just as the buyers of their rice do.

PART TWO:

AS GOES RICE, SO GOES CHINA

CHAPTER 4

AN ANCIENT MARKET

A group of scientists once visited Iran to learn how Persian carpets were made. What was the combination of material and craftsmanship that produced something so heavenly on the floor of a Bedouin tent? What skills, what chemicals and dyes, what traditions and secrets were involved? They grilled the rug makers with questions. And after those scientists left, the artisans went back to their craft of rug weaving and found that something was lost. Having shared with the scientists the secrets of their weaving, passed down from their ancestors, those particular weavers could not longer recall how to weave any more.

It's a story told to me long ago by my father, Fowler Hamilton, who was a student of the world's cultures and a renowned litigator and the first director of the Agency for International Development under President Kennedy. In 1961, he was the highest-ranking person in the U.S. Department of State. My father was a personal advisor to five U.S. presidents, starting with FDR in the 1930s. It is a parable to me of why we fear cultural and business change.

There is that fear in Asia that if you turn farmers into scientists or business persons, the art and the ancient culture of growing rice will be lost in translation. If technology transforms a farmer's practices, people believe, he will no longer truly be the guardian of an almost spiritual way of life that has endured for untold generations, and that's a way of life that must be protected. What many people see is a system that has long worked. It's not broken, they say, and it is beautiful. I understand. I have seen thousands of rice fields, and my eyes never tire of the miracle.

I do see glory in the rice fields. I have stood on the high plateaus of Bali and beheld the stair-step rice paddies flowing down to the Pacific, shimmering like a finely woven fabric. It has seemed to me that those fields must be one of mankind's great achievements, probably even greater than the Great Wall, because those impounded fields are alive, and growing, and feed people. The wall was built to protect. Rice takes floods and turns seed into grain to feed millions. Rice can grow where nothing else would grow. Rice is an aquatic crop.

The fears run deep that an esteemed culture will unravel and change forever, and that traditions that date back millennia will vanish in an onrush of crass, profiteering business. It's also a fear of not having enough. I want to make it clear that helping those farmers will not detract from anyone's wealth. When we promote abundance, we do not ourselves become poorer. If farmers do not own their land

and trade, do not own their markets and their customers and trade, someone else will step in and fill the power vacuum.

Loss of identity seems to be one of the greatest fears holding back Asian agriculture. In my 30+ years as a rice economist and entrepreneur, I think I have identified what the raw fear is. It's not a fear of being hungry. It's not a fear of cadmium in the rice. It's people's fear, rather, of losing who they are, without the traditions of their ancestors. They fear that knowledge of new ways will mean that something will be lost in the fabric of their families and society.

Rice is not just in the mouth but also the heart of many Asians. In the small apartments that rise toward the skies in Hong Kong, most have these two things: a small statue of the God of the Earth, and a rice cooker. People may be living in the city, but the tradition of the earth and its rice is embedded in their memories and culture. It gives meaning to life and makes them part of something greater than their workaday world. Even the very poorest households have rice cookers.

The irony is this: What truly threatens the fabric of society is the lack of constructive changes. If Asian agriculture remains medieval and feudal, people will starve in this twenty-first-century world. Doing nothing is what threatens society now.

THE LESSON OF THE CEMENT IN THE GREAT WALL

One of Asia's great empires was the Khmer culture in Cambodia, which built the great Hindu temples of Siem Reap. The stones of those temples, precisely placed to endure an eternity, required no cement to hold them in place. It is a nearly endless façade of figures swaying gracefully on the seamless stone.

In the other great civilization of ancient China, however, architectural savvy went beyond temple building to the construction of a Great Wall to protect the people from the Mongol hordes. Under several emperors, the wall rose and stretched over mountain ranges and vast distances. Some estimate the wall's length as 5,500 miles or more. It is actually the "Long Wall," not the "Great Wall" in Mandarin.

I've been both to Siem Reap and to the Great Wall. The reason the Great Wall endures is the cement between the stones. It could not be built like the Cambodian temples, without cement. It had to conform to the variable terrain, for one thing. And it was a machine of war, not a place of worship.

In October 2005, I ran a rice conference in Beijing. The premier of China actually spoke at the conference, which is an indication in itself of how important rice is there. At the conference, some rice traders from Bangkok approached me. They wanted to take me on a trip, though they didn't say where. It sounded intriguing, and that afternoon they ushered me out of the hotel and into a van.

I had a fleeting thought that I might never see my family again, but I did know the company that these gentlemen worked for, and so I felt reassured that this was a legitimate outing. I did get the feeling that they were trying to teach me something. Perhaps I'd said something that showed a lack of humility about rice. To this day, I don't really know what their motivation was, other than to show me that rice is much bigger than I thought it was. If that was their objective, they more than succeeded in teaching me a lesson about rice.

"Ah, the Great Wall!" I said as the van approached it.

"Yes," one of the brokers said, "we're going to take you up on the wall." And under the auspices of these rice merchants, I was marched up onto the Great Wall, and with a lot of huffing and puffing. It was very steep in that area.

One of them pointed to the face of the wall. "What's that?" he said in a loud and satisfied voice.

"Those, my friend, are big stones," I replied.

"No, not the stones," he said. "What's that between them?"

"Cement?" I ventured. He added with a bit of frustration, "But what is the cement made of?" I realized I was about to hear a rice fact that, as a world expert, I had never considered.

I tried to think back to my college chemistry class: Let's see. What is cement made from? Does it involve limestone? I didn't have a clue how the Great Wall's cement was made. I'd figured that cement was cement, as anywhere else in the world. And as I pondered the matter, I felt a sense of amazement, for indeed, neither earthquakes nor weather nor war have defeated the Great Wall. It endures after all those centuries.

The rice trader looked at me. "Let me tell you what the cement is made of! It's made of sticky rice and ash from burned rice hulls. The entire wall is held together with rice. Did you know that?"

I conceded that I did not. I felt humiliated. I hardly felt like a world rice expert at that moment. I felt that I was high up in a world that I didn't really even know. And possibly we all must feel that humility, all of us who deal in rice in whatever ways. Its history is ancient, beyond recorded history, and the cultivation of rice is a great achievement of mankind. Rice, basically, was invented in China. It deserves our utmost respect and awe. If we are what we eat, rice is Asia. Like the invention of nitrogen, without rice, there would be a lot less people in this world today. If you like people, that is a very good thing.

As I learned later, there was a legend that the wall was held together with rice, but it was only in 2005 that scientists identified the organic material and proved that the cement was made strong by rice. Then in 2010, it was proven that the amylopectin in the sticky rice was the magic binder that made the cement so strong bulldozers had trouble knocking down the remains of ancient ruins constructed with this cement.

What other secrets about Asian rice remain to be taken out of the realm of legend and be proven by science? I suspect I will spend the rest of my life learning all the things about rice I have so far overlooked. We should never stop learning about what we think we know. It is the humble who will inherit this earth, not the proud. Farming can give someone humility about what we can and cannot control, such are the forces with which farmers contend.

That trip to the Great Wall was how I came to realize that I did not have a clue about some things concerning the rice market. I may have a lot more to learn about the rice market in Asia. I must be open to that possibility. Nobody knows everything about anything.

This is the lesson that struck me so vividly that day. Without the rice cement between those stones, the Great Wall would long since have fallen to rubble. Rice is not merely another grain. It is more than politically and militarily strategic. Rice is the cement holding Asian culture, its history, and its markets together. When the rice in that cement shakes or crumbles, walls and cultural barriers will come tumbling down. I think we will see a time warp in the next decade, as medieval peasants transform into twenty-first-century farmers.

Remember this: As goes rice, so goes China. And as goes China, so goes the rest of Asia. As I said before, 500 years ago half the world's wealth was in China and India, but it was immobile. Now, the Asian agricultural industry is in flux for the first time in history, and China is the leading player. It is the largest consumer, producer, and buyer of rice in today's world market.

Rice is central to the Asian culture, and that culture is beginning to change. In the USA, some people are generations removed from farm life, but in Asia, the city dwellers for the most part are children or grandchildren of farmers. Asia is where the United States was 50 or 60 years ago, when a great many people still had their fingers in the soil, or their fathers did. All that has passed. Now agriculture is food in the supermarket.

RICE: THE "FIRST GRAIN"

So how did rice become man's best friend?

According to a legend that the Chinese recount with a delightful combination of whimsy and sincerity, this is where rice came from: It seems a dog wandered into a flooded village. The monsoon rains had washed the other crops away. A peasant noticed some plants entwined in the dog's fur, and the plants had not perished in the floods. They were alive. He plucked them green from the fur, and the peasants planted them in the mud around their village—and up came rice.

In the United States and parts of Europe, a good deal of rice is fed to dogs, completing the circle of that legend. Rice is one of the most digestible foods in the world for dogs. In the USA, it is also fed to babies and old people at the end of their lives. In Chinese legends about food, it is not so much who discovered something as how it was discovered. Humor creates some humility and puts a human smile on the history of food.

Rice indeed does thrive where nothing else can thrive. It's an aquatic crop that is very productive and can survive deep flooding. Other grains perish in floods. That makes rice a unique grain, particularly in the area of Asia that has, at the same time, dire water problems and too much rain. Rain comes every year and sustains a lot of the rain-fed rice agriculture of Asia, yet until the introduction of rice, people would starve when the rains got too heavy.

China is trying to plan for the future of rice and its huge water needs. The south of China often gets too much rain, and the north too little, so the government is building a massive waterworks to move water north. Called the South-North Water Transfer Project and costing an estimated $65 billion, it is being built to pipe 45 cubic kilometers annually northward along three routes. Still, this project may not solve the water scarcity, and some fear that the melting of snow in the Himalayas will reduce the major river flows nonetheless, diminishing the value of the project.

There's a reason for the hundreds of millions of rice farms and it is the adaptability of rice. The water that floods the fields is a natural weed controller. There's a reason rice can feed about half the world's population. It's a wonderful grain. There are at least 140,000 types of rice, maybe more. It comes in every color of the rainbow. It can grow on dry land, like wheat; in the steep hills of the Banaue Rice Terraces in Ifugao, the Philippines; or it can grow in deep water in Thailand, where it's called floating rice. Man adapts because his rice adapts.

That's why rice is called "the first grain." As the Chinese proverb proclaims, "The precious things are not pearls and jade but the five grains of which rice is first." In Mandarin, "the five grains" refers to cereals, and rice is the king of the cereals. One might think of the grains bought and sold in the world markets and the contributions that the world's civilizations have made to the feeding of mankind: rice, wheat, sorghum, barley, corn, potatoes, cassava, the grains from the four corners of the earth, from Mesopotamia in Asia to Africa to the New World. One might think of the globalization of agriculture generations ago, long before the World Wide Web arrived, and just marvel at it all.

In Mandarin there's a greeting: "Have you had your rice today?" I can't think of anything in the West that would be the equivalent. In the USA, people are fortunately so far removed from starvation that greetings are unlikely to be based on one's relationship to what people eat for breakfast. But the Mandarin expression underscores the importance of rice to the culture. It's as if the greeting said: "Have you been nourished today? Have you beheld the beauty of the paddies from the hillside? Is your heart still in the rice land? Do you know that when you boil your rice, the water is your life?"

In Asia, as people move into the cities from the countryside, they feel orphaned from the farm. They do not regret leaving the poverty and the hard work, but they do regret leaving the world of their ancestors. They still dream of owning land and of reconnecting to their rural roots and the farms that feed people. In our deepest dreams we all dream of farming. I have met many sophisticated market commentators who dream of returning to the Good Earth.

We are all descendants of farmers, and some remain nostalgic about where they came from. They want to be part of the action of soil, wind, sun, and rains again. The cities seem second best to some.

RICE FUTURES AN ASIAN INVENTION

The rice futures market, like rice itself, is actually an Asian invention. Contrary to popular opinion, rice terminal markets did not start with the hedge funds in New York City or the pit brokers in Chicago.

Long before Chicago existed, the Japanese began trading a forward market in rice in 1603. It's disingenuous to say that this marketing invention is a Western product being forced upon Asia. The idea was reinvented in Chicago one and a half centuries ago. Asia has a significant tradition of forward markets, and the first one was rice. Today, rice futures in Asia have fallen on hard times because the central authorities have either banned rice futures as speculation, or have stabilized the rice price through massive stock piling and very high farm support prices.

Interestingly, the inactivity is peculiar to rice; other grain markets in Chicago are priced actively within Asian markets and have local futures markets in several local exchanges in Asia. Rice is simply not managed like other grains and oilseeds. The system of rice farming and pricing in Asia needs to change.

Commodity futures are more than a speculative vehicle; they represent the wealth of agriculture. They allow production to increase with the proper storage and distribution so that the crop doesn't spoil. In the headlong rush to be self-sufficient and grow another 100 million MT of rice, Asia has overlooked the daily task of the grain business.

Rice futures are therefore not the enemy of Asian markets. They are old friends of rice marketing; according to an adage among Chicago brokers, "the trend is your friend."

"WHEN ELEPHANTS FIGHT, THE GRASS SUFFERS"

"When elephants fight, the grass suffers," my rice farmer friend, Jackie Loewer, once told me as we talked about the rice situation in Asia. Think of the elephants here as the large regulatory entities that drive the mindset behind Asian rice prices. When they begin thundering about, they trample the very grass that feeds them. Eventually, the elephants too may die because of their disregard for the grass, the rice farmers.

A society whose rice markets trample the farmer's economic freedom to do business is dysfunctional. A healthy and dynamic state gives its farmers full support, and by that I do not mean price supports, but rather, a healthy state equips farmers to use technology, develop markets, run the business of farming, and teach their craft to their families and those who will inherit their small businesses. It takes a lifetime to learn to farm in a particular manner in a particular place with particular resources. We must preserve that know-how. Farmers must be mentors in order that we might better feed the millions, and the urban billions.

CHAPTER 5

TECHNOLOGY'S PROMISE

Today's technology explosion and access to information has lain the foundation for a more liquid and transparent rice market. Never in history has information been so accessible, and it offers the education that farmers need to compete in the urban labor markets and the marketing mechanisms to price what they produce for a profit if they wish to stay and farm.

Armed with technology, the rice farmer has a renewed capacity to make sound decisions from the bottom up, in effect, doing what he did for centuries before the implementation of the modern, top-down management of the rice price, largely after World War II.

With the changing climate and changing markets of today's world, it is time to put as much responsibility and market freedom as possible into the farmer's hands. We must bring the market to the farmer, and those who are in between the farmer and the consumer should have to justify their existence.

THE PROMISES OF TECHNOLOGY

The fertilizer for profitable agriculture is marketing education and the application of technology. Cities are where the universities are at and cities are where the grain exchanges are located. Digital communications take the space and distance out of agriculture and turn markets into a place to go and trade, every day and every night. The business prospects ahead could be truly amazing for the food grower and the food consumer.

We have talked enough about our fears for now. I am in awe of what our millions of rice farms could contribute to the world's wellbeing in just the next seven years:

> The Net is allowing us to turn ourselves into a giant, collective meta-intelligence. And this meta-intelligence continues to grow as more and more people come online. Think about this for a moment: by 2020, nearly 3 billion people will be added to the Internet's community. That's 3 billion new minds about to join the global brain. The world is going to gain access to intelligence, wisdom, creativity, insight, and experiences that have, until very recently, been permanently out of reach. (Peter H. Diamandis and Steven Kotler, *Abundance*, 2012)

Our information age provides rural farmers and merchants with unprecedented access to the markets and to one another, and that raises the hope that significant change could come to Asian agriculture and the way it is marketed. It is time to bring the market as close as possible to the rice farmer and his rice field, and the advances of technology are making that possible. We also need to bring the land market and the farmer together for mutual profit and development. Farmers should have the privilege of staying on the farm or leaving it for the city with some real money in their pocket. That is not yet happening in China. Agriculture that steals land from the farmer is not farming; it is thievery. Theft is the father of hunger and ignorance.

The rice farmer can have the same access to information about the markets that until very recently was only available to the major grain corporations. In China, companies such as the Hangzhou-based Alibaba Group give the promise of regional and national online buying and selling for all kinds of food. The more the middleman's take is reduced, the more money will flow to the producer and the consumer of rice. In the world to come we must each justify our take from the dinner plate and the rice bowl.

Technology will allow farmers to communicate with one another and expand their marketing affiliations and horizons. They will be able to join together, combining skills and resources to respond in a timely manner to the markets. They would have the expertise to know best which crops would be best for the region and for their profit potential. And they would be able, via online education, to gain whatever expertise they lacked.

A major advantage of the technology boom is that it could create more market access of the seller to the buyer, and that is making it easier than ever to root out the corruption in agricultural systems around the world. With the light of technology shining down, it is far harder to make money in the dark. Technology is credited for the declining crime rate in the West. If crime doesn't pay, it starts to go away.

IN A BLINK OF TIME, MUCH CHANGE

The agricultural sector, in China and India in particular, has been stuck in a medieval mode. It has been immobile. Now, in our information age, it can become mobile. It has the ability to be on the move, and that is where it has to go.

You can think of "mobile" as in mobile technology—that is, the ability to communicate easily with other farmers, while they are in the fields, and market the crop in a far broader region. Much of the responsibility that's now being handled by the state can become the domain of the individual farm, or a group or association of farms. Mobility puts world markets and information literally in the farmer's vest pocket.

Until about 15 years ago, access to information in the rice market was extremely expensive and only available to the major grain corporations. Now, those corporations are feeling the heat as everyone has the same access to instantaneous insight as they do. That takes the business down to the farm. Those who work the soil now can have the education and power to become a rice market force. They can act as the major grain companies did long ago. Online access and education transforms the possibilities. The farmer can gain the requisite expertise in the field without the bricks and mortar and libraries of institutions. An iPad now offers 3,000 free educational videos to millions of users and a book, video, and audio library far larger than the U.S. Library of Congress.

In addition, as we shall see, the technological explosion is leading to other benefits in the agricultural system. By promoting digital transparency, it is making it easier to weed out corruption. And it opens opportunities to transfer financial aid directly to the poor, so that society can attend to their food purchasing needs without artificially controlling farm prices.

IS TECHNOLOGY UP TO THE CHALLENGE?

Whether technology can help will depend in large part on rice price support programs. For example, in China, when authorities continually increase the price of rice and wheat, they're not creating much interest in efficiency in the rural sector. They're just getting more for what they grow. They turn the farm markets into farm museums.

What I think will have to happen is that the markets will come to the farm rather than be controlled by a top-down agricultural management. It would be similar to what happens in Brazil, Russia, and the United States with other row crops. The farmer must become a technologically advanced market manager and not a lifestyle or subsistence farmer.

THE POWER OF FARMER ASSOCIATIONS

The technological vision for the Asian farmer includes the potential to set up free-forming farm networks. The power of technology will better equip farmers to join together to share their smarts, and to network voluntarily. One person is good at marketing. Another is a tech wiz. Somebody else is a soils expert, and there's a guy who's good at logistics. The sales and marketing type can move the product into a wider channel as the farmers do their job in the fields. In this way, a one-hectare farm can form a 1,000-hectare marketing pool. I'm not talking here about collectives; I'm talking about voluntary associations, one of the greatest assets of American business. These associations are not imposed from outside; they grow up from within the nature of the local markets, their topography, and geography. They may or may not be like U.S. farmers' cooperatives, which are large and institutionalized.

It's hard for me to imagine every farmer being an independent hedger of his grain in Asia, for three reasons. The first is the lack of exchanges, education, hardware, and software. The second is the small size of the plots that grow the food. The third is the mindset held by many in government positions that free markets in rice that offer forward pricing breed excessive volatility and speculation.

An association of farmers creates a transitional ground in Asia until farms can become much larger. It pulls farms together and creates a larger base of production so that the farmers and the social rice network gain sufficient power to become a market force. That is done through technology, education, and enlightened regulation.

To me, a farmer cooperative (co-op) is part of the answer to the agricultural problem, not just in less-developed countries but in developed countries, as well. In the USA, there are all kinds of co-ops. There are input co-ops. There are processor co-ops. There are rational reasons to have a co-op that markets grain inside an agricultural system, but it need not be all or nothing: A farmer could sell some of his production to a co-op and keep some back to price on his own. A co-op should not be a club, but just another way for a farmer to make money. If it underperforms relative to the market, then simply cut the co-op out of the farmer's marketing program.

The kind of co-op that works best, in my judgment, is one in which people may or may not be a member. They market some of their grain through the co-op and some on their own. The analogy is in stock trading. You may buy some of your own stock and also have a mutual fund or ETF that handles some of your investments. You're continually comparing the two and deciding which is best. On-farm storage is also an important tool for getting the most money for the crop grown, at least for part of the crop.

There is too much doctrine and ideology in the marketing of crops. Let the market determine who survives and who doesn't.

Of course, some farmers don't care about understanding the food markets. They just want to grow the crop, and that's where specialists can help with the marketing. There will be, in every area, people who can operate on behalf of the farmer to deliver the crop to the marketplace. They may or may not physically buy and sell their rice. For specialty products, it is very important that the farmer be able to shape his production to the demand. As urban incomes rise, as the emphasis changes from food security to food safety, and as agricultural products become customized and specialized, farmers' profits should increase. Recent studies indicate that customized production of nearly anything adds as much as 67 percent to profit margins.

A HYBRID SYSTEM FOR ASIA

I am envisioning a marketing system, not totally Western nor totally Asian, yet moving out of state-controlled and state-mandated farm prices. Pricing freedom can create something more flexible.

In this world of drones, smartphones, and 3D printers, the sky is the limit on agricultural change agents. That includes the possibility of some agriculture moving into city buildings. Urban farming could become a hydroponic and multi-floored growing center, referred to by some as "vertical farms." Technology and rising costs for water inside cities is making it possible to implement many new ideas never before possible, and those innovations need to be managed by well-trained people who are comfortable with a smartphone and iPad and understand the markets, supply and demand, and how grains move. And they will want to be paid for what they do.

According to the Food and Agriculture Organization (FAO), an estimated 800 million people worldwide are engaged in some kind of urban agriculture, producing 15–20 percent of the world's food. That percentage should only rise over time as farming reinvents itself inside and outside the city. Populations will urbanize and so will some of their food sources.

If there are upwards of 200 million rice farms and there are at least five people on each farm, that is 1 billion people. There may be upwards of 1 billion people living on the millions of Asian rice farms, and they feed 3 billion people. So the ratio of rice farmer to rice consumer could be as low as 1:3. Over the next 30 years, that ratio will have to increase to 1:30 or 1:50, as in the United States. How that ratio changes will depend upon what kinds of things those farms are doing in 20 or 30 years.

Perhaps one valley, two valleys, or a whole province could work on behalf of the farmers to produce more and create more profit. In that way, the many small farms can function as the large farms do in the West. You can turn thousands of hectares into a marketing entity where the interest of the entity or network is to maximize the profit for the farmers within it. In biology, it is called the principle of swarming, freely forming networks for mutual profits and market strength.

EASIER TO WEED OUT CORRUPTION

The technological explosion also has made it easier to weed out corruption in the agricultural system. Aside from the layers of legitimate rice brokers and traders between the rice farmer and the rice restaurant and rice bowl, corruption steals money from the producer of grain.

Technology, which supports transparency, can advance the cause of marketing freedom for the farmer, as well. It turns every one of us into a market force. It puts the farmer's finger on an iPad, literally, and turns it into a global market force to buy and sell and price his crops.

The visibility of the electronic platform in 2006, for example, removed some inequitable floor trading practices of open outcry in Chicago. It leveled the playing field quite a bit, especially for the farmer.

Prior to electronic grain trading, the runners and the pit operators had an edge and saw more of the market than did the customer on the phone. Now prices and volume offered or bid are there for all to see. They are what are known as the "waterfall." The mechanism of electronic price discovery eliminated the practice of "fast" markets where, during a market shock, a customer on the phone had no idea when or at what price an order would be filled. Usually, it was the customer off the floor who got the short end of the price spread. All farmers are off the floor but can be present online.

Electronic trading has its detractors and its own problems but capacity to handle large contract volume is not one of them and the cascading and visual stream of the bids and offers are evident and can be taken out at any time by a farmer or a trader for a global grain house. An online and electronic platform increases liquidity and volume and puts a farmer's finger on a keyboard and in the middle of global price discovery. What is wrong with that? In this way a feudal farmer can become virtual, digital, and profitable.

DECIDING WHAT IS GROWN AND WHERE

It can be hard to predict what lies ahead. Visions of urban farming may seem far out to us now, but such techniques might come sooner than we imagine. Everything may be grown like fresh vegetables, even rice. Everything may be sold with a pedigree and certificate of origin, especially for wealthy urban restaurants and consumers.

As water quality deteriorates, supplies diminish, and costs rise, we will find new ways of dealing with the conversion of water into food. Agriculture of this coming century could be a cross between a Saturday morning farmers' market and a customized supermarket. Anything that is expensive is well sold with good service to back up each transaction for the grower and the eater of the food.

For the time being, however, governments will still be edgy that not enough acres are devoted to some crop that they deem necessary for self-sufficiency. To free up farm prices, they have to allow for yearly changes in crop acreage. In 2013 in the United States, for example, because of market signals, cotton acreage was down 20 to 30 percent. Peanut acreage was down hard. Bean and corn acres were up strong, and rice acres were down. That has to happen, not just in the USA but also across the Americas, where relative farm prices drive a farmer's planting decisions. Relative prices, not state planning goals, need to drive production. That is why, along with good water resources, the West feeds the rest of the world.

In the north of China, except for very high support prices, acreage is more likely to shift between crops, where several crops can be grown, as is the case in the Southern rice region of the USA and in Brazil. Those farms are going to grow what the prices are signaling. Yet even now, the Chinese government is creating most of the price signals, so the country continues to grow more and more wheat and rice. As a result, those crops deteriorate in quality and spoil, with related problems of ground pollution and storage issues, such as mold or aflatoxin.

The best way in the long term is to let the acreage and prices move with the world market. China needs to grow crops and reward farmers, as happens in Arkansas. I say this knowing that in vast areas of Asia, farmers will grow rice come hell or, literally, high water. It's an aquatic crop that does well with the heavy rains of the southern regions. In irrigated areas, however, farmers need to be able to adjust crop acreage up or down. Rain-fed agriculture will remain cheap but irrigated agriculture will become more and more expensive over time. That is where water costs will escalate.

The food price scares in 2008, when rice prices screamed to $1,000 per metric ton in Vietnam, have altered the mindset of many across the rice-growing world. But when plans are based on fear rather than on economic opportunity and the promises of technology, agriculture becomes dysfunctional.

AN AGRICULTURAL NETWORK

I believe in online rice information and social networks. They're starting to crop up in farming. People who are separated by time and space can ask simple questions that large grain companies used to ask. If there is a crop failure in a certain country, do I know someone there who can cooperate or give an opinion on it? With a mobile phone and a social rice network, that can be done. A network is two people on a text message or 2 million people trying to get the market story straight in their own minds for their own wallets.

The goal of agricultural networks online is to allow people anywhere—farmer, merchant, processor, or broker—to network with one another. Greek rice farmers might talk with Australian farmers about how their crops are doing. Networking builds valued relationships, which over time builds trust. Trust is what is sorely lacking among the rice players of Asia. That is part of the reason why regional rice reserves are a nice idea with no takers.

Social networking allows people to connect with strangers from afar and create the kind of friendships and connections that large international agricultural companies now enjoy. It takes the world down to the local level, levels the playing field for farmers and puts market force onto their farms. People in any rice-growing area of the world can communicate with those in other areas and compare notes, not just about the market but about technology and best practices.

PART THREE:

THE TRICKS OF THE TRADE

CHAPTER 6

THE VISIBLE HAND OF PRICE CONTROL

When it comes to rice, the nations of Asia for decades have rejected economic philosopher Adam Smith's concept of the invisible hand of the market that regulates prices for the common good. What the world has seen, particularly since World War II, is the quite visible and very heavy hand of government controlling the price of rice. In the fast-paced world of commerce, it has been the most protected and immobile commodity price, and rice remains so today.

Over the decades, regimes from democracies to communism to fascism to socialism have felt the need to control the price of food grains, and rice has been chief among them. This culture of control has been made possible by the increasing wealth of Asian nations. It takes money to implement market controls.

Government intervention was virtually unknown if you look back a thousand years. In the Thailand of that era, anything could be bought and sold on not exactly a free market but a disjointed open market. Starting with the establishment of the Iron Rice Bowl in China over half a century ago, all the way to the present, governments increasingly have feared fluctuation and volatility in the price of rice.

A CULTURAL RELUCTANCE

A major reason for the lack of an open rice price in Asia is the central role that rice has long played in the society. Rice is social and cultural cement, and it is nearly sacred to the older generation with close ties to the farm. We explained this aspect of rice earlier. However, to the youth who have left the farm, that faith in rice has eroded to an agnostic view of rice as a food commodity, with no particular difference from wheat, corn, soybeans, or meat prices. As fewer and fewer people remain on the farm, that characteristic of rice will fade. Obviously, per capita consumption of rice is sort of going down and diets are diversifying. Rice is a slow food and an old way of eating.

It is an old man's view that rice is sacred. It's not so much the view of a young person in the city who is so much better off and feels insulated from what created such fears in the minds of the previous generation. Yet, Asia remains closer to the low incomes of the Great

Depression than the United States. People in positions of power there have known hunger and financial destitution. In the West, hunger isn't known to the same extent. Once you don't know hunger, your whole view of the agricultural sector changes.

Most other grains and oil seeds have moved toward open markets. Their market volume has mushroomed recently. Governments, however, exercise control in markets besides rice. Obviously, they intervene in the currency markets. So free and open pricing is a relative term, but on a scale of 1 to 10 for control, rice is a 9+ for control and the other commodities are 4 or less.

Because rice is produced locally and consumed locally, governments can have a great deal of control over the ability of the market to price rice. The Far East has mostly an anti-futures and anti-speculation mentality.

Governments can't control gold, currencies, or share prices, and they can't control iron ore. They can't control coal, and they can't control crude oil, although in the scheme of things, the cost of energy is much more significant than the price of the grains because of the energy spent to produce them. We are a hydrocarbon-dependent society. Gone is most of the animal and human muscle power of a century ago. And yet rice still trades as if plows were pulled by water buffalo.

A FUTURES MARKET'S THREE ESSENTIALS

In the West, grain markets trade somewhat freely, perhaps in large part because they have forward markets, largely located in Chicago,

Illinois, at the CME Group. They also have trustworthy regulatory bodies to enforce the rules of the financial game on its players.

A forward market needs three things in order to grow: a buyer, a seller, and those market makers called speculators. In my world, speculation is not bad. Speculation gives farmers a chance to sell during the year at higher prices, and it gives buyers an opportunity to buy at lower prices. Notice when the speculators gang up and drive rice prices low, we do not see anybody in the world press complaining that the rice price is too low. Low rice prices do not make the newspapers and are good for what ails a market and high rice prices are bad. That is at least an assumption of non-farmers.

The other thing that speculators do is to create liquidity for merchants to lay off risk. It's sort of like the people who buy a life insurance company to make money on the actuaries' guesstimates of risk. They try to figure out the potential of price and trends in price spreads and make money. A speculator may not realize it, but he is in the actuarial business. He is in the price insurance business for someone else. We should hug a speculator, not run him out of town if the rice price turns bullish and increases in value.

Small towns in Arkansas are prospering in a way they hadn't before because they have rice merchandising functions there in addition to farming functions. Since rice futures came to the Delta in 1986, a farmer can have a price every day for his rice. He may not like it, but it is there to take or leave.

When I came into the industry in 1981, the farmer grew the rice and gave it over to the government, just as in Thailand in 2013. The government piled up many months of unwanted rice stocks. Those stocks either deteriorate in quality or move through the system because of the cash rice brokers and merchants. Rice merchants hire people and create wealth within the small towns.

This merchant trading is a way to make local regions more prosperous through storing and pricing to buyers what the farmers sell. Because no other rice futures contract is active anywhere else, everyone watches it like a financial North Star for world rice, which of course is a bit absurd. U.S. rice futures are merely a price to buy and sell rice in the tiny state of Arkansas along the Mississippi River. Few farmers use forward market pricing directly. Rather, they take advantage of pricing through local rice merchants. It is the merchant who retains the line of credit to handle the multiple moves in prices.

The cement for the U.S. rice industry is not the sticky rice that holds together the Great Wall but that silent business function in which sophisticated merchants, while seeking their own gain, are able to bring money back to their communities.

That's what Asia desperately needs: the aid of the free markets, not top-down prices from their governments. Good grain markets are built on the sturdy, unexciting job of getting values right each and every day of the crop year. The merchandising workhorse, not the politician, gets the local job done of moving rice through the system from the rice paddy to the rice bowl and the cafeteria.

THE UNIQUE NATURE OF RICE

Wheat, the sister food grain to rice, has taken a very different course of development. It operates as other markets operate, with liquid forward markets and a sophisticated and well-financed marketing chain. Rice trades as milled or processed rice in world trade. Wheat trades as the raw product harvested from the farmer's field. What would a rice market look like by 2050 if it had a market like wheat?

Local wheat markets around the world price off the Chicago terminal market for a variety called soft red winter wheat. That's just one among many kinds of wheat, but basically the linchpin price for the entire wheat world comes out of Chicago for that variety. There's a historic precedent for that. All you need is one world price, and you can key other markets off it.

We have many wheat markets around the world, with many varieties, just like rice. They are local and domestic markets, and in the end they key off of Chicago because that's where the liquidity is. The market goes to the source of liquidity, not necessarily to the most representative quality or quantity of the commodity or even the biggest grain producer or consumer. Most primary commodities find a price based on the raw product as it comes out of the farmer's field, such as soybeans, or the other grains.

Until the agricultural investment boom of the last 30 years or so, these U.S. grain markets were just local in delivery areas and function. They were started in Chicago in the 1850s to take care of the fluctuations in supply from harvest through planting in the Midwest. Today, wheat has one world price, with discounts and premiums based on quality and origin. The risks are spread out because of that. All the big grain companies use forward markets to reduce risk, not increase risk. To some people, a futures market might look like a casino, but in truth it is more like a Lloyd's of London for grain movement. A futures market spreads risk and allows farmers, merchants, and buyers to take a small business margin out of their activity during the year.

If wheat were merchandised internationally, as is milled rice, it would all be traded internationally as wheat flour. The rule of the rice market is that it is controlled by the local rice millers and by the exporters in Asia, not by the farmers or farmer cooperatives, as in the USA. That is why most rice is priced and sold as milled; the added value of the coproducts is kept within the country. That is also why nations want to buy whole, unprocessed wheat to keep milling jobs inside their domestic markets. Very little paddy or rough rice trades internationally unlike wheat and unlike wheat, rice moves from areas that grow rice to areas that do not grow rice in large quantity such as the Middle East and, to a lesser extent, Africa.

The wheat processing produces not only byproducts but also wheat milling jobs. Central American countries are an exception to the rice rule and buy U.S. rough or paddy rice for the same reason; it keeps milling jobs at their domestic mills in Central America and it keeps their control of the domestic distribution chains. Most countries grow wheat. However, just a few countries in Asia grow most of the rice globally. So most rice importers want milled rice not rough rice, as they historically lack rice-milling facilities in their countries.

A hundred pounds of rice will produce about 10 to 11 pounds of bran. That's what's on the outside of a brown rice kernel that people prize because it is more nutritious. There are about 20 pounds of hulls. The remainder is white rice; some either is broken, semi-broken, or fully broken. The hulls have some value as an energy product. The bran is an animal feed ingredient or is used in some health food products and for rice oil extraction. If the bran has the oil taken out, it is called defatted bran and is more stable than fatted bran.

Centuries ago, the Europeans brought white milled rice technology to Asia; similar to the white milled wheat flour they produced at home. After Asians gained a taste for milled rice, nutritional deficiency developed in children and their diet had to be altered. Brown rice is, in fact, the perfect food. Another near-perfect food is beer. You can almost live on beer or brown rice. Many in the USA consume most of their rice in beer. I have no great taste for brown rice, but I do like beer. Aside from pet food, one of the largest industrial uses for rice in the USA is beer making. For health reasons, brown rice is making a come back in the West and for good reasons. I will drink to that!

There is another fundamental difference between wheat and rice trade. Generally speaking, rice consumption is very much as it was hundreds of years ago. Unlike all the other grains, rice is put on a plate and eaten as it is grown. It doesn't have a strong industrial sector, other than beer and some use in pet food and feeds. It's a very immature market in terms of alternative industrial uses. It remains a slow food in a fast-food world. Rice is eaten largely in the form it is grown. If the cooking characteristics, or the aroma, or the milling characteristics fail to please buyers, they will walk. Another term for the cooking characteristics of rice is the "mouth feel." Rice consumers consider themselves expert at the rice they eat and can be very picky about what they will buy.

A lot of wheat is eaten as a chip, on the go, as a bun, or whatever forms of munchies the fast-food industry cooks up. Rice is boiled in water. No other grain, aside from oats, is eaten, generally, as a boiled whole grain. The only way you can wrap your mind around rice is to imagine that all the world's wheat is boiled and eaten as it is, the way some grains are in Africa. In fact, all other grain commodities and oil seeds are crushed, extruded, or reduced to flour. Rice is largely eaten as a whole grain, not extruded or recombined. Rice is WYGISWYE, "What you grow is what you eat."

My belief is that eventually a great deal of the world's rice will be eaten as fast processed food rather than slow food. It may take a generation or two, but it will become part of this highly processed world that comes with income gains. A bowl of hot steamed rice is not made to grab and run. But with rice milk or ice cream in a cone, rice cakes, crackers, or chips, you do not need a fork or chopsticks, just your fingers. Rice fries, by the way, are rather full-bodied and quite tasty. The problem with rice is it generally costs more than potatoes, so do not expect MacDonald's to stock rice fries anytime soon.

For 18 years every day at 11 a.m., I would sample what I had bought and I would sample rice cuisine from across the globe. I was grateful I bought rice, as I love to eat rice.

What I bought as the company rice buyer I had to eat as well. I was very concerned about the quality of what I bought for that reason. You might call me an expert rice taster as well. I have eaten samples of every rice dish known to man and from every origin in the world through our company's R&D Kitchens. I am no stranger to rice.

You can see that rice is a poor man's food. It's slow but convenient. As milled rice, it's ready to eat. You bring wheat into a port and it still has to be milled. It has to be baked into flatbread or yeast-based wheat products. Rice is immediately ready to eat. You take it from a bag, and you put it in a pot and boil it. Ironically, it is, in a sense, the world's first convenience food. Yet it is not part of the fast food, highly processed world that exists today for the other grains.

Rice is the first grain in Asia. Its history has also made it a unique grain, highly controlled, and closely watched over by governmental authorities. No other grain is bought and sold internationally almost totally as a processed product. Soybean meal and oil do enter world commerce, but they are a small part of the raw soybean market that is bought and sold between countries. This makes a world forward pricing market or an over-the-counter contract particularly challenging because it would have to be for milled rice, most likely.

THE ACCESSIBILITY OF FOOD IN INDIA

Open markets make the food business more efficient and more profitable to all. The chicken industry in India is the model to begin to implement in Asia, along with the Wal-Mart model for distribution. The goal is less waste and spoilage. Nations don't have to double their rice production. They need to halve their rice losses.

A recent study by the International Mechanical Engineering Association indicated that 20 to 80 percent of all the food grown in less-developed countries is lost before it gets to the wholesaler. That's where they can increase food supplies: by reducing corruption and waste and spoilage before it reaches the wholesaler. That can only be done through private business. It can't be done through governments. Food spoilage is a result of flaws in the marketing chain and/or consumer preferences.

It is clear that the people of India are becoming wealthier and demanding more food safety and more specialty products. India is a vegetarian society that has been able to "get by" as a vegetarian society, but that is slowly changing as it moves toward the consumption of chicken.

The nation is a democracy but remains an enigma in many ways. A binding force there is actually the English language, which reaches across different cultures and languages, but India is complex and no one understands that country well. It has an excellent business culture, but does the government have the political will to solve its resource problems and not compound them?

Those who cannot add value to the process need to step aside. The appearance in India of companies such as Wal-Mart could help rationalize and make more efficient the Indian food marketing system.

India, as an economist said recently, needs a free trade agreement with itself among its own provinces. It is in such sorry shape, not in terms of producing stuff, but in terms of marketing, storing, and providing accessibility to that food, and that's just as important as producing more grains and more rice.

RICE FLOWING FROM THE WEST

Rice, which was discovered and developed by the genius of the Chinese people, will eventually be sourced to some degree from the Western Hemisphere. That is my prediction, based on the assumption that areas with problems of shortage of clean water will buy from areas that have nearly limitless water and a favorable climate for rice, such as Brazil. That is when the societies begin to realize their water is precious and they cannot have both shortages of water and farmland and be self-sufficient in food grains.

I predict that the world 20 years from now will see the Western Hemisphere as a major provider of rice at much higher global rice prices than currently exist. Why will the price be higher? It will be higher because the cost of water and farm inputs must increase tremendously in Asia as economic and physical conditions force subsidies to be unwound.

South America is a food pantry to the world. It can grow whatever the world needs and can pay for. The Mississippi Valley can produce more rice, but it too is limited on water resources. In Mississippi and Arkansas, controls haven't yet been placed, but people are concerned about water supplies.

Does this sound unlikely, rice from the New World? I would point out that soybeans were discovered in China but are grown now and exported to Asia from the New World. Potatoes and corn were discovered in the Americas but have been grown in Europe and Asia. South American rice production has increased tremendously in the last decade. For centuries, foodstuffs have been globalizing our world. Food markets do not stand still.

Long after the United States owns a smaller share of the world rice trade, it could still have an Americas rice contract, based in Chicago. If this happens, the Chicago contract could become like the wheat contract. It could become a world benchmark for prices. A lot of change has to happen in the world of rice in the interim, a lot of obstacles already discussed must be overcome. In particular, rice has to move up to or beyond the cost of production in the USA and South America, which is about mid-point between the Indian, and the Chinese rice price today. That will only happen because of a shortage of water and nontoxic soils to grow it in Asia.

Instead of declining in value relative to the other grains and soybeans, as has been happening since the late 1990s, the rice price would increase in value relative to other grains and oilseeds. The feed grain prices have expressed the need for protein and biofuels. Rice will express, eventually, the cost of water. Rice, hydrologically speaking, is twice the cost of wheat or soybeans.

Some believe rice production will become obsolete in the Western Hemisphere. That will only happen if water remains a free good. Few realize that rice goes all the way back to the early colonization of the Americas by Europeans.

The Americas have been growing rice for centuries, since the days of Cortez, in Mexico and Brazil and later in the British colonies, particularly South Carolina. Rice growing and indigo dye made Charleston, South Carolina, rich. And the rice crop continues to flourish in the West. The Western Hemisphere, mostly the South American nations of Uruguay, Argentina, Brazil, and Paraguay, will continue to produce rice and respond to the world need. This is not a forecast. This is virtually a certainty. How we get from here to there is a great uncertainty and depends on the market pricing of water, not rice directly.

In Africa, at one time, rice was called "Christmas rice." That was because folks there could only afford rice for Christmas. Now they can eat it every day of the year and do so. Life is getting better for all of us, despite what we hear from the doomsayers. We have a lot to look forward as more serfs are freed from the slavery of abject poverty and move into modern cities.

THESE THINGS WILL COME TO PASS

"The future belongs to the learner," wrote the social philosopher and longshoreman Eric Hoffer, "while the learned will find beautiful ways to cope with a world that no longer exists."

Many rice support programs are very complicated and very learned but are simply not part of the change to come. They are learned attempts to cope with a world that is vanishing before our eyes. I do not profess to have all the answers to society's ills. In Chicago, when all else fails, you follow the trend.

The world is changing digitally at the speed of light, and we need to unstick rice markets from a pricing world that no longer exists.

In another sense, however, the process of change is slow and grueling, despite the fast track of technology. The only viable futures market for rice is in Chicago. It took 32 years for the U.S. rice market to develop to a level where it amounts to just 1.7 percent of world rice production.

You don't need a lot of a commodity with a forward market to impact and benefit the world, but I do not believe that the rice contract in the USA is yet a world market. I think someday it could become one, if the changes in the Americas come to pass. Yet, every time the price of rice rises in Chicago, you hear the predictions from the press that people are going to starve to death because they won't be able to pay for Chicago rice futures. That to me is utter nonsense.

It may take a doubling of exports from the West to solidify Chicago futures as a world contract. Thai, Vietnamese, and U.S. rice prices must begin to move as one across the rice globe.

The two hemispheres, East and West, are disconnected in their rice pricing for the time being. India is separated from China and both are separated from the West. Japanese rice prices are very high and disconnected from other markets in Asia and the West. There is not now a single rice price as a reference point. Wheat is the grain of the West and rice is the grain of the East. Someday wheat and rice will trade similarly and rice prices in the East and in the West will merge into one, global rice market.

You have to get the rice price out into the digital light. Online trading, with market price discovery, is an important part of that. Forward market pricing brings to an archaic, splintered market the fire of change.

CHAPTER 7

THE FUTURES OF THE
PAST AND PRESENT

L et me make something perfectly clear to everyone. Chicago grain
futures and Las Vegas have little in common. Grain forward
markets were not started to create volatility for the benefit of
speculators eager to make money on price swings. The U.S. casinos
are in Las Vegas, not Chicago. Futures markets are transparent and
global. What the futures price says does not stay in Chicago. It flies
around the world at the speed of light.

Grain forward markets were started to solve seasonal volatility
and a lack of credit to finance grain trading. Did you know that the
Federal Reserve Bank was not just set up as a response to the panic
of 1907 or to promote the banking industry in general? In the USA
back in 1913, when the USA was more agrarian as is Asia today,
it was established also to assist and smooth out the seasonal credit
demands from the grain industry. It was also intended to promote
mortgages to farmers. So agriculture in the USA was initially one of
its strategic purposes.

Studies of such markets consistently show that they level out
market fluctuations and credit needs; they make markets less volatile.

They reduce the incidence of bankruptcy. There is simply no economic validity to the perception that they increase volatility.

Such was the purpose in setting up the market in Chicago when the nation was still very much in touch with its agrarian roots. The first grain contract traded on March 13, 1851, in Chicago. It was a corn trade. Now 162 years later, I am urging consideration of trading rice in Asia just as wheat and corn were traded in Chicago a decade before the American Civil War. Prior to corn futures, farmers had been getting low cash prices, to the point of bankruptcy at harvest time, while later, the price would soar. The original purpose of grain forward pricing was not to award the speculator a Powerball lottery win but to allow grain to be harvested and stored and then distributed during the year.

The United States has had huge increases in yield and volume of its grain crops since 1913, with changing requirements on storage and credit, even in the last 50 years and even the last decade. They've all been managed because of merchandising from forward prices discovered in Chicago. The USA and Brazil have become the grain pantry for the entire world. It's that merchandising function throughout the year that holds together the U.S. grain market and keeps the focus intently on the market. Brazil grows its own beans, but it borrows market liquidity and merchandising expertise from Chicago. It is the lack of that function in Asia that is causing quality problems for stocks as food grain production soars higher.

The United States has market and subsidy defects, of course. The USA subsidizes crop insurance rates, but unlike in Asia, the U.S. Farm Program doesn't try to intervene directly with high prices or low prices for the grains. Also, the poor in Detroit do not riot when soybean prices triple. Neither do farmers in Arkansas riot when the soybean price is cut in half.

U.S. grain markets in Chicago have succeeded in their goal of creating less volatility and less seasonal price change, and that accomplishment was largely at the hands of private firms and farms, not the federal government. The grain quality standards came out of Chicago and not Washington, DC, for example. The federal government is a late arriver to the U.S. grain markets, which were sleepy little affairs, like Asian rice, until the foreign nations finally grasped their importance, hedging buys and sells in the world grain markets and the need to use hedging to reduce, not increase, price risk over time.

CHINESE INITIATIVES

Changes to the world and domestic rice markets could come with increasing speed. The hands of the great clock of innovation move ever faster each decade now. A market change such as the U.S. rice futures, which took 30 years to come about, could now be accomplished in five years or less. The Chinese studied the U.S. market in forward rice pricing very methodically and for some length of time before implementing it inside China's borders. China is getting it right but slower than I would prefer. In fact, in 2013, that project seems on the edge of failure, due to its contorted support price mechanisms. The U.S. futures nearly died for three years between 1983 and 1986 for the very same reasons that the rice market is stagnant in China and Thailand today.

As we already mentioned, the Chinese have a small contract in early rice paddy futures and now at the Zhengzhou Commodity Exchange (ZCE) there is a move to start trading a japonica or medium-grain contract, the kind of rice eaten in northeastern China, the Koreas, and Japan. China reportedly produces about 65 million MT of japonica rice, which dwarfs production and demand in the rest of the world. Japonica rough rice commands some of the highest prices for rice outside the aromatic markets.

The Chinese have limited volume trading because of high price supports for domestic long-grain rice. The rice futures market is barely alive, like a small candle flickering inside a jar, but it is not yet the lighthouse of rice price discovery.

At least in principle, however, China has gone through that painful process and has come out the other side. Other countries in Asia might wish to study what China has developed with its paddy rice markets. As goes China and rice so goes Asia.

TWO HUGE POPULATIONS FACING FARM CRISIS

Unless attitudes toward the farmer change, the situation could become critical in less than two decades, with major implications for world hunger and rural poverty. In India and China, two huge populations are facing an agricultural water crisis, even as their grain production escalates year after year. China, in certain areas, is letting the cost of water rise and beginning to get some control over water use. However, India is basically giving water and electricity away for very little charge to farmers. When you do that, you don't have any market price allocation, and you lose efficiency.

India has little control over water use right now. Office holders need the farm vote, so they lack the political will to change water regulation, despite public concern. In China, only about 7 percent of the land is arable; in India, it is closer to 54 percent. But that doesn't mean the water situation is any better in India. Each year, India consumes about one-half of a Lake Mead amount of groundwater. Lake Mead is the largest man-made reservoir in the USA. Lake Mead, by the way, is suffering a drought that has been in play for 10 years in the southwest of the USA. Unlike debt or paper currency, a government cannot just simply manufacture more groundwater that it is not there. Land must be both arable and have access to water to grow food.

China has a population base in its interior cities alone that is the size of the entire U.S. population. Those interior cities will develop farmer markets into supermarkets. Who will remain on the farms that feed those supermarkets and where will the water come from to grow all those food stuffs, from which mountains and from which rivers? No rivers, no farming, no farmers, no food.

PART FOUR:

"YOU CAN'T FAIL"

CHAPTER 8

GETTING STARTED

Governments must agree to lift their hands off the rice price and the marketing chain and to allow the rice markets to evolve under private ownership. In rice commerce, "profits" and "merchandising" and "futures" must become good words, not bad ones, for the people and the regulators. If there is no profit on the farm, there will be less food for the cities.

That is not to say that we let the "invisible hand" take complete control of the rice market, because regulatory supervision is needed to avoid problems that can develop as individuals handle money. The regulation would be similar to that in the United States: an agency would oversee warehouse law and exchange integrity for the clearinghouse, which is necessary under a forward market. Crooks are an endemic problem in any governmental or commercial system. Asia needs an electronic rice contract and a clearinghouse that ensures that financially solvent companies back the prices and trades and that all threat of default is eliminated. Effective regulation is one secret of the financial magic that is the futures markets.

All of these elements would be handled as top-down financial regulation, but not as top-down pricing. Regulation keeps people honest but does not dictate how things will get priced. The marketing goal is to make the rice price transparent and allow it to fluctuate with fairness and accuracy.

Another term that is so negatively viewed in Asia, rice price "volatility," is necessary in order to find the resources and to allow the private sector to breathe financially and take profits. You will not have a private sector to market if there are no profits. We need to move beyond the idea of a "tranquil" rice price. Is the gold or crude oil price particularly tranquil?

That's the problem with Asia. It has had a spectacular success rate at focusing resources on increasing production, but not on the logistics of storage and developing the farmer as a merchant or a professional seller.

You don't just pile up or push money on the rural sector to reduce the Gini coefficient (which measures income-level distribution in the population, with a lower number, meaning greater equality). A Gini value of zero means perfect equality. Thailand has shoved up rice prices to push income into the farming sector. Such hoarding methods of creating a stable society will fall of their own weight.

Agriculture is not just about growing more and pumping up input subsidies or prices received by farmers, but it is also about turning farmers into educated, flexible, and entrepreneurial professionals. They are not gold prospectors; they are rural innovators who will show all of us the way to a well-fed and better life. Successful grain markets are a dull, everyday affair to move food up the marketing chain from rice paddy to rice bowl. Governments should focus on market regulation, not on price manipulation to win votes or raise rural income.

Buying rice from the world market should not be viewed as a sign of agricultural failure; it is simply another grain pantry for rice procurement. A more vigorous world rice import and export market means these countries have more virtual water resources to dip into in a climate crisis and alternatives to feed their people, not just through domestic sources.

International buying and selling of rice is already a market-based reserve stocks idea and can turn desperate situations, such as we experienced in 2008, into positive growing situations for the whole food sector. Hopefully, rice trade will increase from its current 8 percent of world production to more like 23 percent, which is the level of world wheat trade. World rice trade should become a supply buffer for weather accidents inside individual countries, not a dumping ground for overproduction.

JUMP-STARTING THE DREAM

There are basic minimums to making a vibrant rice market inside a country for paddy or rough rice forward pricing. First of all, the government needs to be hands off, at least partially, on the matter of rice price volatility. Second, the government needs to be hands on when it comes to exchange regulation and financial integrity. There's a role for regulation in government, but not as it is now being performed in Asia. Third, there has to be a pool of companies willing to provide the backing for trading, a clearinghouse for Asian rice.

There need to be champions for this market: financially solid companies on the buy and the sell side of the market. Someone has to start and build the market at the beginning. It took 30 years to create a rice market with forward pricing in the United States. My former employer was one of the founding members, along with a couple of other very large grain companies, and the big farmer co-ops. We all put the orders in every day and took on the risk of illiquidity. Nothing starts without money involved, and it takes business courage to put your money on the line in a new market. A journey starts with the first step, and all markets build one contract at a time. Liquidity is in the eye of the beholder. All grain contracts are "thin and illiquid" to a foreign currency dealer.

These are the kinds of players who need to be courted when starting up a contract. Every day, someone has to buy and sell the market. In rain, sleet, sunshine, and gloom of night, every day the market has to find willing firms to price rice. Someone has to deliver the daily mail, so to speak. There has to be open interest, which measures the size of the market, and there has to be contract turnover or contract volume. A successful and vital commodity market has in its backbone commercial buyers and sellers of rice. There is no other way. Commercial players bring speculative players to the market, not the other way around.

The missing element so often overlooked by market pricing "projects" like this is education. Education is essential for merchants, for rice farmers, and for government regulators to understand what this thing called *forward markets* is and is not. I list educational resources in the appendices for aspiring merchandisers and exchange organizers.

The education needs to be done through in-house and online classes, which are available. The online element of the world today allows education to flourish and grow at a reasonable cost to users, who can master the markets in the privacy of their home and on a laptop or an iPad.

Grain futures work best in a tradition of successful merchandising that exists in several countries, such as Brazil and the United States. Generally, there is less of a grain merchandising tradition in the Far East. A market is not just for either buyers or sellers. It's about getting together at a price, every day, and now every night, electronically, with your fingers pushing the trading keys.

The financial safety of the clearinghouse is essential. Even before the Great Depression, no forward pricing market has been closed down in the USA because people ran out of money. There have been lots of problems with financial entities, such as stock and credit markets, in last century. That is one reason I advocate an Asian rice futures experiment in Singapore. Singapore has the integrity, the financial wherewithal, and the interest to start up a contract. The world has changed dramatically since 1981 when the U.S. rice futures started in New Orleans, Louisiana. The sheer amount of wealth and the ease of starting an electronic pricing platform are the fertilizer for success.

The world rice market of 2013 is drenched with news and prices that are easy to access over the World Wide Web. A decade ago, that was not the case. Successful markets tell a market story 24 hours a day. Rice now does that very well.

It takes courage to start a new commodity market; few have ever experienced such an effort, as the origins of Chicago grains are lost in the distant past. I was fortunate to be part of the start-up and development of the Chicago rice contract in 1981. I was also fortunate to be mentored by someone who was instrumental in starting up energy futures, Michael Marks.

Michael Marks, former chairman of the New York Mercantile Exchange, was a supporter of a commodities advisory and trading company I started back in 1980. He was always bending my ear about the potential for crude oil futures, which at that time was just an idea in Michael's head. I asked him once, with some skepticism, "When would your crude oil contract be in the big time?" I thought he would tell me, "When the Seven Sisters accept it." No. He said, "When Houston does not buy or sell crude until our New York price opens up." It is not where something is priced but who will put their money on the line and use it in their commercial dealings. Big markets often start up with little businesses taking up the dare.

In those days, the biggest thing in energy market trading was New York heating oil, bought and sold on the exchange by small jobbers around New York City. Big changes start with tiny markets in a few, brave people's heads.

Now the reason I mentioned milled rice is because crude oil did not start trading as crude oil. The large oil firms, the Seven Sisters as they were called, at first did not want to be involved in developing price discovery. They liked things as they were. They made the oil price happen. Like international rice traders, they didn't think anything in energy was broken. However, Michael, fresh from the failure of the potato contract, did see a unique opportunity for his exchange. In the beginning, he was the majority of the ownership of the heating oil futures market. At the beginning of rice futures trading, I also might own up to 50 percent of the rice forward market. I used rice futures as a hedging tool for a large, annual rice purchase of hundreds of thousands of tons of paddy or rough rice.

I think the rice markets are broken. Michael thought the energy markets were broken or, more specifically, were a new opportunity for his exchange. He mentored me in the early days of contract development, as he was an expert in facing into disbelief and selling the world on a new way of trading. Michael did not write the book on energy; he traded it.

Similar to the Arkansas-based U.S. rice contract today, small merchants started heating oil contract trading and had no vision for saving the energy industry. They just wanted to make a buck along the Hudson River, and that's where the energy forward markets were born, not in West Texas or London or Singapore. Rice futures began trading along the Mississippi River as a paddy or rough contract. Many of the founders of the U.S. contract were just public-spirited rice farmers with other side businesses, such as warehouses and trucking firms. New York energy contract trading migrated to London and then the world.

Arkansas delivery, rough-rice, contract design migrated to China but so far without much success. Again the deal killer is high, immobile rice-price supports, well above world-traded prices, inside China. The same is true in Thailand.

There are lots of ways of starting forward contract trading, but the goal is to see active, online trading, with integrity and a financial clearinghouse for every key, paddy-market area in the world, such as Bangladesh, Indonesia, possibly the Philippines, China, India, Thailand, Vietnam, and Pakistan. All these countries should embrace and develop local terminal markets that then can be connected by the Internet over time. It's a local project with global implications.

I have this vision that someday there will be a website somewhere in this world with the prices of rice flashing continually 24/7 for the benefit of those who drive the rice marketing chain, the rice restaurants, and the rice farmers. And those prices will light up the rice world across Asia. Government regulators will keep the crooks out of the deal flow and their hands off the price flow.

It's not how large the supply is but how enthusiastic and well financed the players are. A small market can become a benchmark. Again, a small part of world wheat is in the soft red winter wheat area of the US Midwest, but that price is the benchmark with premiums and discount to almost every wheat market around the world. It's an Illinois River-type market that has become a global market by default. Everything goes to the liquidity, and the liquidity is at the CME Group in Chicago. The Mississippi, Illinois, and Hudson rivers can be the birthplace of a new world of agriculture, if governments and major players will just release their grip on the price of rice as they once did for energy. Crude migrated to the Thames River in London and rough rice could migrate to the Yangtze or the Yellow River in China.

CHANGE COULD COME SWIFTLY

Were it not for the technological wonders of our information age, rice market change would certainly come slowly in the future. It took three decades for rice futures to take root in the USA.

Were it not for the Internet and electronic trading, all these ideas could take another 30 years for any of these countries to get going, particularly considering the prevalent negative views of open market pricing. Big journeys begin with the first step.

In this day and age, however, everything's going electronic; everything's going to forward trading, and everything's going global—except for rice. Therefore, what took 30 years back in 1981, for a tiny contract inside the USA, could take less than a decade to come to pass in Asia.

Strangely, in this world of trillion-dollar markets, the most underfinanced area of the world market is agriculture. The most backward, unsophisticated, and unprofessional part of the world financial markets is agriculture. In the old days, when production and demand were static, you could do that. Now everything is in motion, particularly grain production and populations. People are leaving the farm at the rate of 20 million to 30 million per year in China alone. The figures are reportedly similar in Africa. Talent is exiting, not moving toward, the Asian rice farm. People are getting older.

Will the last man to leave the rice farm turn off the lights in the grain shed?

Asia needs to turn the rice sector into profit opportunity instead of a social burden, and stimulate its activity and finances. Financial arrangements need to move into the rural sector, and swiftly. Technology is compressing time. The rule of thumb has been that in this age, seven pre-Internet years have become one digital year, but I have a feeling that exponential things are going on underneath the surface that are further compressing time. That's bad news. If nothing changes in the rice sector, people will not be able to eat. We do not eat virtual or digital things; we still eat real tangible rice. Even in this age of online innovation, 80 percent of the dollars in world commerce are still spent in the physical part of reality, not in the digital world. Successful industries connect up the physical and the digital worlds for more profitable arrangements.

As the cost of water goes up, it is time for preparatory action.

CHAPTER 9

STEPPING FROM THE SHADOWS

I believe in the human spirit, with an unassailable optimism that things will get better, not worse, that we must not fail.

No one started out to make life hard on the farmer. In fact, government-set rice prices are like those elephants stomping the grass. Still, the monolithic pricing system is failing the farmer. There is growing pessimism that there is no other approach other than the current one.

There are many ways of approaching rice farm programs; some intervene in the price and others that just distribute money such as in the USA. What is the best way to help the farmer run a profitable agricultural enterprise?

Many of us are simply afraid of going broke and ending up hungry in the poor house. When you have a negative mindset about the farmer, based on fear instead of on opportunities, what you hope to avoid may sadly come true anyway. There will be loss of production, loss of farmers, and loss of ability to react to escalating change. Businesses fail for fear of change more than for lack of courage.

To be a success in business, you need to be an optimist who is realistic. To succeed, you need to manage your fears and expect not to fail and know why you won't fail. Studies show that 80 percent of businesses failures are the result of owners who convinced themselves they would fail before they even started. I never start anything expecting to fail at it. Cynicism is often a cover-up for a fear of failure.

People have to leave agriculture in droves. I know that and you know that. But someone still needs to stay to farm. Will that person be a medieval serf, making $2 per day, or an educated and savvy farm manager who can make a profit? A bright future awaits any agriculture in which the one who leaves does so by choice, not by coercion or poverty.

In the case of Asia, part of the solution might be for those younger people who move to the cities eventually return to the farms, more knowledgeable about markets and technology. But for the youth to return to the farm, there has to be money in farming. "Don't farm, you will starve to death," was the warning when I was growing up.

Happiness comes from financial freedom of choice. The one staying on the farm and the one leaving—both should face a better economic future, a better education. A rice farmer friend of mine, who is a mentor to me, wrote the following prose poem. It touched my heart deeply. It talks about the family transition that will take place hundreds of millions of times in the next two decades in Asia.

This poem speaks to the heart of farmers everywhere. Real life is what happens to us as we make our beautiful or cynical plans. Life is as rough and tough as is the rice that the rice farm grows. The setting here is Louisiana near a farmhouse by a rural road west and north of New Orleans. The time is December.

In the USA, many farm kids go to school in a yellow school bus. Mr. John Hugh was the driver of that yellow bus. This rural setting could just as well be a rice farm on the Yangtze River or the Indus River in Asia. The emotions of change are universal and transcend time and place.

TO MY CHILDREN IN DECEMBER

It's 6:50 a.m.
At the end of the driveway I stop
at the street as the old, cold, rumbling school bus passes,
that same old bus that carried
you to the education that carried you
away
to a world of knowledge, understanding, and caring.
Mr. John Hugh is gone.
Mom is gone.
The children that huddled on that old, cold, rumbling
bus on a dark winter morning
are gone.
But even in that melancholy there is
sweet joy in knowing you are
doing well
being productive
raising another generation
that gets on a school bus that carries it
to an education that will carry it away.

—PAUL "JACKIE" LOEWER, LOUISIANA RICE FARMER (POEM COPYRIGHTED 2013)

My farmer friend, Jackie, who wrote this poem, pointed out to me that his poem is not a melancholic farewell to his children in December. Rather, those are the words of a wise rice farmer who chooses to remain behind while some of his children choose to leave. The greatest freedom, exhilaration, and joy in life are the opportunities to make choices to better our circumstances, either in the city or on the farm.

Education requires wealth and commitment and is a form of preparation for great things and it gives us real choices. Chance favors the prepared mind, and education prepares us. "I will prepare and someday my chance will come," Abraham Lincoln said. Now Asia must see its rice farmers as someone whose chance has come.

THE SHAPE OF THINGS TO COME

There are two views of Asia. One is that all the words that I've used here about rice futures are not good things for farmers' markets—words such as profit, trading, the farming business, or global speculation. To some mindsets, these are negative and pejorative concepts that get quoted in the world press. Others agree with me that these are positive words and build the business opportunity for the rural sector and its farmers.

As farmers move to the city, will rice prices also move toward open market, forward pricing mechanisms? A futures exchange is an urban concept, birthed in Japan 410 years ago and in Chicago, again, 162 years ago. Exchanges trade the farmer's produce but they are urban innovations.

The eighteenth-century economist Thomas Robert Malthus theorized that catastrophe or war would reduce populations growing large and unwieldy, as if people were a trouble to us. But if that were so, what would life be all about? It's either about people or it's about nothing at all. People are a miracle. A major miracle that rejects Malthus's hypothesis is that abject poverty—earning less than $2 a day—has declined dramatically in the last two decades.

There has to be public concern for the poor who are devastated by rising food prices, while also giving the farmer an opportunity to make money through the pricing system.

CHAPTER 10

THE PROSPEROUS FARMER

*The future is not a result of choices among alternative paths
offered by the present, but a place that is created—created
first in the mind and will, created next in activity. The future
is not some place we are going to, but one we are creating.
The paths are not to be found, but made, and the activity of
making them, changes both the maker and the destination.*
—JOHN SCHAAR, FUTURIST AND PROFESSOR EMERITUS AT UC SANTA CRUZ

"It is in God's hands, may we have the courage to accept it."
—MARVIN COCHRAN, A GOOD FRIEND AND A MISSISSIPPI RIVER FARMER
LOOKING AT THE RAGING WATERS OF THE MISSISSIPPI RIVER IN 2011 AS IT
WAS ABOUT TO JUMP ITS BANKS AND DESTROY HIS FARMING OPERATION

Weather and climate are the constant companions of the farmer but will he have the flexibility and the personal courage and education to meet those challenges in Asia? Will those who control and regulate his markets have the courage to put the big decisions back into the rice farmer's hands?

Can the Asian rice farmer, toiling on a farm he does not own and stripped of any market force, become prosperous? Is the vision here not better than today's uncertain future? Do we really believe we are creating our future by our mindset and will? Mankind creates most of our problems, so mankind should have the solutions to the problems within its grasp.

The Chinese word for *crisis* (**危機**) contains within it the word *danger* and perhaps a hard-to-translate word, *critical* or *crucial point*. Perhaps we are at a *Kairos*, a Greek term for the right or opportune time. A woman says the baby is coming and the man looks at his smartphone and says that it is not due for two more weeks. The woman, not the man, is right. She means the time is "now!" Her body is on *Kairos* time. That is how I see the days and years ahead. The dangers ahead are obvious and a bit bleak, but this point in time is crucial and unique in human history. With preparation, there could be a happier outcome, not a more dangerous outcome.

If you're going to consider that everything I've proposed is wrong, you're going to have to convince me that the status quo is working. If the status quo is working, I need to know in what way it is working. Huge social and technological change is coming down on our heads, with migration and rapid aging of the farmer population. We have swelling migrant populations in the Asian cities. People of higher income there are demanding food safety and other things that the system can't easily deliver. It's an obvious business opportunity for the farming sector and its support lines. The word "NO" can mean to some, "New Opportunity."

The path we're on may turn out to be heartless, but people no longer respond well to heartless. They rebel against it. Freedom is where the people of the world are headed, from the brave fruit vendor in Tunisia, Mohamed Bouazizi, to the toiling farmer who will not eat the rice he grows because it is not fit to be eaten.

"Are these the shadows of things that will be,
or are they shadows of things that may be, only?"
—CHARLES DICKENS, THE CHRISTMAS CAROL

I don't believe in fatalism. The future is created first in our minds and then worked out through our beliefs about mankind. No shadows of what is to come are a certainty, and often reflect our fears, not reality. I believe in personal choice, and I believe that the way to a better world is by striving for a successful future. We can succeed in agriculture in two ways. We can endure a long period of starvation and mass exodus and unemployment that will eventually rectify itself over time, or we may wish for something much better at this crucial point in time. We can advance beyond all that, logically and progressively, on the strength of Asia's rice culture. We have the vantage point of seeing past urban migrations that failed for everyone who endured them. These decisions are not in our hands, but perhaps I have persuaded you that the powers that be should make a way to bring together the best of Asian grain markets and markets in the West.

Rice is profound. Words do not convey the miracle of life that rice has given to the human family. I believe that city dwellers still have a heart for the farms, for the rice community. They want safe and abundant food, and they also want to connect with the roots of where they and their forefathers came from. Rice is the food of their ancestors and it takes money to make rice markets happen.

They remember the land and its earth gods; they see the rice cooker every day and are grateful they can eat what is grown on the land that their fathers and forefathers loved. In Asia, people are much closer to their farm heritage than are people in the West. In the West, food has come from a supermarket for at least two or three generations. In Asia, it's still the vivid memories of mother and father, grandmother and grandfather, toiling away in the rice paddies. Rice is still a family thing and a land thing.

Hunger is something that Asia's managers and directors and department heads understand far too well. The West doesn't understand it as well, and that is because of so many successful years of feeding people.

Finding markets for farmers' rice and giving them the proceeds of the land they farm is not the answer to hunger or social unrest, but I hope it can be a small step for a more humane future. Our small steps add up to progress, and I hope that at journey's end will be a world of fuller stomachs and far less ignorance and want.

"YOU CAN'T FAIL"

If you start a small company such as a farm or a firm, you need to understand basic business principles. I've never farmed much as a way of life or as a business, but many farmers take our service. My wife is the daughter of an Iowa farmer. My own father was a farmer and a lawyer. In our home, we are one generation removed from the farm.

I understand the plight of those who run small businesses, because I have one. I've been successful in three businesses over the last 13 years in an environment that has not been totally friendly to what I do.

I thought I had the answer back in 2000. My business partner, Kevin, and I had a dot.com idea at a time when the world was folding in the cards on dot.com investments. I was depressed and was trying to find money so that I could make money.

As I stood outside the office of a venture capitalist in Houston, Texas, one day, I felt an invisible touch on my left forearm, and I heard a voice of a young man in some godforsaken rice field in Asia whispering in my ear, "You can't fail! You can't fail!"

I suddenly realized that all that I was doing was trivial compared to what that young farmer was enduring. I wasn't making much, but it was much more than $2 a day. A great deal of the world struggles to have enough to eat for the day, to have shoes, clothing, and shelter for its children, much less a secondary education. That's not true for me. I had money, a good education. I had food, clothing, shelter, and the blessings of a Western economy and agriculture that had treated me very well. I could get some other job or retire.

I realized then that what was driving me was not a basic need; it was a desire to do my part to change the rice world. That young man's whisper was not telling me, "Your efforts will succeed in changing the way in which the world trades rice. You will be a success some day." No, rather, he was telling me that my hopes and dreams would certainly come to pass. These changes, he was saying, are inevitable. Whether I would be involved personally or not wasn't the point. What I desired could not fail. It will come to pass.

My meeting that day with the wealthy venture capitalist did not go as I had hoped. "You're going to do well, and you're going to make money," he told me, "but don't get us involved. We don't understand your rice business. It's not our money that you need. You need customers."

My thoughts often turn to that young Asian farmer who tapped my arm. He doesn't need subsidies and venture capital. All he needs are customers, food consumers and their restaurants willing to pay well for what he grows. That farmer cannot sit back and wait for his smartphone to jingle in 2020. He needs to reach out over the Internet, or have someone in his group or association do it, to find markets and to respond to those markets and give people what they want to eat. Sellers need to learn to sell what they have and go out and find buyers willing to pay for what they want to sell. That is what real business people do for a living: they go and find customers and buyers to whom they can sell.

A farmer needs to learn how to sell. He is a seller by virtue of raising a crop, but he needs to learn to sell, in the sense of stimulating demand. That is what a successful businessperson is, someone who sells, stimulates demand, and manufactures and delivers the goods and services in a timely fashion. The United States has that kind of farmer, particularly in the high-value markets. That kind of farmer is starting to appear in Asia, with specialty rice over the Internet. That kind of farmer will help us all eat, feed, and succeed, and enjoy the great blessing of an abundant and secure life. He is the restaurateur of the food marketing chain, welcoming visitors to his farm and asking, "What can we serve you today?"

TIME FOR REFLECTION ON WHAT THIS ALL MEANS

think there's a place for the idea of transforming the rice market into a wheat market in this century within Asia. The wheat market is more or less one price. The rice market can similarly become one price. China probably discovered rice thousands of years ago. Japan invented rice futures in 1603. Chicago stumbled upon futures in 1851. U.S. rice futures began in New Orleans in 1981 and then moved to Chicago in 1986.

Asia just needs to release the genius of the nearly 1 billion people living on rice farms to deliver from their fields safe and secure food, not just more grains. We need a "meta-intelligence" of abundance for rice as 3 billion more persons across the globe step onto the Internet by 2020.

When rice shakes the world, the economic map of little white grains could reshape itself. In Asia, the obstacle is rice and yet the way is rice. This is not my forecast. This is a crisis and a certainty.

Permit me to tell you a personal story. When you use markets as a commercial player, you're going to have losses in your forward account, but you may well have gains in your cash account when it is marked to market. That's the most difficult thing for accountants to understand, because all they see is current money flow. The physical purchases of rice do not generate daily gains and losses like the futures. Again, success is all about educating all the players.

I was in a big debate with the CFO of the rice company I worked for at that time. A brilliant man, he brought me into a room and chewed me out privately and said, "What are you doing by losing all this money in the rice futures markets? What are you trying to do here?" I looked at him and said, "Well, I'm not exactly doing that." I tried to explain how grain hedging works. And then out of my mouth came something like this, "Since you asked, I want to change the way in which rice trades globally." He looked at me and said, "That's a tall order!" I agreed. And I hadn't even known that I wanted it until I said it to him that day. Over the years, I have bought millions of metric tons of rice, real and on paper. Now my customers are the ones who do that. I advise them and they trade.

A lot of things in life come to us unexpectedly: someone taps your forearm, or you blurt out something that could jeopardize your job.

At times, you must think with your heart and speak with your heart. You need to speak up about your convictions and in what you believe, whether others agree with you or think you are a nut. This book is not the last word in rice markets. I want it to be the first. I want people to be able to express what role they'll play in the transition from medieval agriculture to twenty-first-century rice marketing in Asia. It's an exciting proposition. It's not a dire or desperate one at all.

Does the Asian rice farmer deserve better access to rice markets? That's the question I pose to you. We must get the conversation started. Our world is changing rapidly. I would like to suggest some specific steps that people could try if they are in a position to change local Asian markets and wish to help find that better way for the farmer not just to grow but also to market what he grows. Pass this book along to anyone who is tired of broken and dysfunctional rice markets and is in a position of being an agent of change. The following are some of these suggestions that could bring together the East and the West. Some of these suggestions can be done by individuals inside countries now, whatever the current rice policies there might be.

- Support the formation of local futures and more transparent physical or cash rice markets across Asia with regional values. Do it with the hope that they would become interconnected over time into one global pricing mechanism. That would help people determine when to grow their own stuff or when to buy it from someone else. As is the case with all human commerce, the first questions to ask is, "Should I make it or buy it?"

- Conduct education for every player, from corporate accountants to regulators to farmers, to commercials, to government officials, to politicians through online courses in merchandising and hedging of grains. Nothing changes without education and retraining. The farmers, in the end, should become professional sellers, and professional sellers are merchandisers. Farmers need to be able to read the market much better than they can now. We need to provide the farmer and the buyer of his produce the best marketing tools with which to operate. The world probably needs fewer brokers and more merchants, people who will take real positions and take care of real inventory rather than people who have a phone and just call up and try to buy stuff from other people. After all, every farmer in the world now has, or soon will have, a smartphone in his pocket. He may have on-farm storage bins and trucks. Will his rice market be as smart as his phone?

- If you are or know a farmer, tell them to improve their marketing with disciplined economic analysis. Find services that deliver a market story from a neutral or nonpartisan market position such as our service, Firstgrain.com. When it comes to market advice, you will always get exactly what you pay for. Join a rice community on some social network to broaden your market relationships and global awareness. Ask each other questions and ask other farmers and commercial interests in rice for the answers, or better questions.

- Build out smartphone technology for farmers via social networks and trade associations to turn the rice farmer into a professional rice businessperson and rice merchant. It is not enough to grow a crop; you must also harvest the price as well as the rice to prosper.

- For those in a position to launch new rice markets, I urge them to deliver the market directly to the farmer, the one who grows the food. Let everyone in between prove his or her value or get out. No water and clean soils, no rice. No rice farmers, no rice.

From my perspective, the current rice state of affairs in Asia is quite broken and is creating broken people, impoverished farmers who cannot rise to the potential within them; and the next generation is fleeing to the cities, where people may take up a miserable life, orphaned by ignorance and want.

Rice is a great product with a great tradition and a great consumer base, but it needs to be brought into the twenty-first century. I want to put a voice to things that people have whispered to me in the back rooms at rice conferences. I want to be a gadfly on the back of the rice industry, asking, "Tell me why I'm wrong?" I know that people can change the shape of things to come. They have the authority to do so.

If Asian rice countries can implement just some of these recommendations here, we can move toward a better future and a better farm market for everyone. I do not believe that we were ever meant to be hungry and in need and not have enough. We are all meant to live abundantly and have more than enough. The farmer of tomorrow must not be a peasant, but rather a professional.

Agricultural change begins and ends with the rice farmer. Those who live in Asia know, yet many sense a despair that things will never change. In the West, we live on an invisible economic fault line and it is lined with Asian rice. Rice is the cement that holds the Great Wall of Asian society together. If it comes apart due to a lack of professional farmers, both the East and the West will feel the tremors.

We are not just what we eat but also how we grow that food. The rivers feed the cities of Asia and the aquifers of Asia and those waters sustain the annual rice crops. The nature of sharing the waters as they come down from the mountains creates a certain society of cooperation. In the Midwest of the USA and the Middle East and Europe, most wheat fields are reliant on rain. Perhaps this is one reason why the USA and the West focuses more on the individual, whereas Asian society begins with collaboration and cooperative enterprises.

There is no crop in the world as reliant on cooperation as is rice in Asia. I hope that this tendency for cooperation will overcome other darker forces of control, domination, and conflict.

If you got nothing else from this book, I hope you understand a little better why rice could shake the world. In the end, I hope rice will help, not shake it, and, thereby, create a better and more innovative future for all of us that live across of this vast and varied planet.

PERTINENT LINKS FOR EDUCATIONAL TRAINING AND RICE INFORMATION

1. Firstgrain is a global rice advisory service that publishes the weekly newsletter, *The Firstgrain Rice Market Strategist.* Its customers include farmers, millers, traders, and finished rice buyers. This book's author, Milo Hamilton, is its Senior Economist.

   https://www.firstgrain.com/default.aspx

2. Papers and viewpoints on Asian rice futures at the RFM Meeting, March 22–23, 2012, in Singapore:

   A. Milo Hamilton's position paper on Rice futures:

   http://www.rsis.edu.sg/nts/resources/db/uploadedfiles/
   SubmitttedPositionPaperonFutures.pdf

   B. Full Report of the Expert Working Group Meeting on an 'Asian Rice Futures Market':

   http://www.rsis.edu.sg/nts/html-newsletter/report/
   pdf/RSIS_FutureRicePolicy_300812.pdf

3. Rice price and news services with coverage of U.S. rice futures:

   Oryza is a daily news and price reporting service that is published on line both in English and Spanish for the world rice industry. It includes monthly summaries of rice activities by country and region, as well as ongoing recaps of key activities in research and marketing related to rice. It also publishes The Oryza White Rice Index.

www.oryza.com

Live Rice Index (LRI) is a leading provider of benchmark price assessments in the rice industry. The LRI's goal is to increase transparency in this opaque market, enabling all rice market participants to make more informed trading decisions, whilst limiting their exposure to risk.

www.livericeindex.com

Creed Rice Co., Inc. is an international rice brokerage firm whose core business involves origination and sales of rice to and from several countries around the world. We also write a weekly rice report...the Creed Rice Market Report, as well as maintain the leading rice portal on the web.

https://www.riceonline.com

Coastal Rice is a rice marketing firm centered around gathering information, analyzing, offering opinions and advice, and assisting growers in executing trades in cash and futures positions.

http://www.coastalrice.com/

4. Rice Futures Exchanges

CMEGroup:

http://www.cmegroup.com

Zhenzhou Commodity Exchange:

http://english.czce.com.cn

5. Online Training in Grain Basis Merchandising at The University of Arkansas:

http://globalcampus.uark.edu/Special_Programs_and_Professional_Studies/Professional_Development/Grain_Basis_Trading.html

6. IRRI: Asian Rice Farming Research

The International Rice Research Institute (IRRI) is a research and training organization. This non-governmental organization (NGO) was established in 1960 to develop new rice varieties and rice crop management techniques. Its goal is to find sustainable ways to improve the wellbeing of poor rice farmers and consumers. It has offices in 16 countries.

http://irri.org

7. What 250,000,000 people in China migrating from rice farms to cities looks like from on high:

http://www.nytimes.com/2013/06/16/world/asia/chinas-great-uprooting-moving-250-million-into-cities.html?_r=1&

ACKNOWLEDGEMENTS

I want to acknowledge those in and outside the rice industry that have inspired or mentored me over the years. Some have been instrumental in the writing of this book. Some are no longer with us but have left their mark on my heart. I have not distinguished between the living and the dead for that reason. This list includes rice breeders, rice traders, sales agents, coop managers, millers, processed rice buyers, business owners, farmers, regulators, exchange and U.S. Department of Agriculture officials, professors, and others who have helped further the global dream of a better way for the world's rice farmers:

My father, Fowler Hamilton; John and Forest Mars, who gave me my first job in the rice industry; Andy Morris; Jim Rogers; Tom Miller; Simon Constable; Sameer Mohindru; Pat Daddow; Mark Creed; Jay Davis; Stephen Jones; Ben Savage; Thomas Slayton, Dr. Peter Timmer; Jeremy Zwinger; Jackie Loewer; Marvin Cochran; Randy Ouzts, friend and business colleague, whose company, Horizon Ag, inspired the cover of this book; Gene Kunda and David Amato, CFTC regulators; and Ralph der Asadourian, former CFTC regulator; V. Subramanian; Duncan Macintosh; Mike Verdin; Sameer Mohindru; Sally Trethewie, Singapore-based economic consultant; Dr. Ramon Clarete; Dr. Sam Mohanty; Dr. Bill Tierney; Dr. Andrew McKenzie; Dr. Bert Greenwalt; and Dr. Eric Wailes. I want to thank Joe Crane, fellow world traveler, friend and rice farmer; David Van Oss; Vichai Sriprasert; Mr. Pradit of Mahboonkrong; Frank Gouverne; Mamadoo Ciss; John Thygerson; Chris Bonneson; Sal Amram; Hu Wenzhong; Zelin Zahao; Pham Quang Dieu;

Shahid Tarer; Kim Hein; Nelson Mucenic; Tiago Sarmento Barata; Lee Searle; Hank Clark; John Lynch; Dave Masonis; Drew Lerner; Joel Widenor; Jack Scoville; Ed Taylor; Matt Dilly; Stuart Hoetger; Dwight Roberts; Betsy Ward; Denis Delaughter; Bob Papanos; Dickie Hollier; Martin Simon; Grover Connell; Jay Kapila; Robert Dubois; Ricardo Hahn; Charlie Pinto; Jac Luyendijk; Steve Bresky; John Lestingi; Gene Martin; T. J. Thompson; C. Ron Caffey; Don Haller; Ray Brewer; Fred Seamon; Keith Glover; John Oakes; Carl Brothers; Lee Adams; Paul Crutchfield; Kirk Messick; Bobby Hanks; Nocha Van Thielen; Dawn Habricht; Elton Kennedy; Brian Semple; Randy McNeil; Gerry Morris; Raymond Murrell; Richard Hastings; Elton Robinson; John Larose, Jr.; Lee Searle; Hank Clark; Bruce Scherr; Tim Price; Bill Chambers; Andrew Aaronson; Nathan Childs; Michael Marks; Merrill Oster; Jim Weisemeyer; Mark Wimpy; Bud Frazier; Cash Mahlman; David Lacour; Fred Zaunbrecher; Roger Tinsley; Dean Wall; Brent Weaver; David Smith; Jacko Garrett; Des Woods; Pam Wostarek; Mark Anderson; Donnie Bulanek; Bob Bisswanger; Greg Baltz; Andy Boone; Robin Boyd; Michael Sullivan; Sam Whitaker; Paul T. Combs; Vernon Thweatt; Richard Hardee; Steve Keith; Ivan and Jean Paul Schepens; Franco Garibaldi; John Owen; Ron Miller; Larry Lockeby; Brian King; Bill Duncan; John Anderson; Ray Stone; Phil Rizzo; John Denison; Neal Stoesser; Greg Simpson; Wendell Walker; Phil Yates; Tommy Webb; Ross Thibodeaux; Buster Bain; Stewart Bundrick; Greg Yielding; John Alter; ER Coleman; Neauman Coleman; Carl Frein; Steve Linscombe; Jim Stansel; Anna McClung; Charlie Bollich; Kirk Johnson; Shawn Hackett; Don White of White Commercial; and my 800 plus connections in the global rice industry on my LinkedIn membership.

I especially appreciate all the many current and former rice farmer customers of Firstgrain, who through the wind, rain, cold, and drought have shown the world how tough are those who grow the rough rice. You all were with me as we wrote this rice book together, and I am humbled to share in your rice and market wisdom.

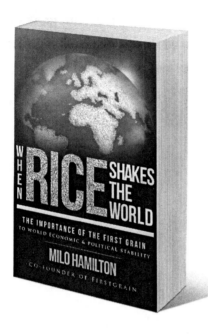

How can you use this book?

MOTIVATE

EDUCATE

THANK

INSPIRE

PROMOTE

CONNECT

Why have a custom version of *When Rice Shakes the World*?

- Build personal bonds with customers, prospects, employees, donors, and key constituencies

- Develop a long-lasting reminder of your event, milestone, or celebration

- Provide a keepsake that inspires change in behavior and change in lives

- Deliver the ultimate "thank you" gift that remains on coffee tables and bookshelves

- Generate the "wow" factor

Books are thoughtful gifts that provide a genuine sentiment that other promotional items cannot express. They promote employee discussions and interaction, reinforce an event's meaning or location, and they make a lasting impression. Use your book to say "Thank You" and show people that you care.

When Rice Shakes the World is available in bulk quantities and in customized versions at special discounts for corporate, institutional, and educational purposes. To learn more please contact our Special Sales team at:

1.866.775.1696 • sales@advantageww.com • www.AdvantageSpecialSales.com

CPSIA information can be obtained at www.ICGtesting.com
Printed in the USA
LVOW10s1940300314

379535LV00005B/7/P